TEACHER'S PET PUBLICATIONS

PUZZLE PACK
for
The Hobbit

based on the book by
J. R. R. Tolkien

Written by
William T. Collins

© 2005 Teacher's Pet Publications
All Rights Reserved

The materials in this packet are copyrighted
by Teacher's Pet Publications, Inc.

These pages may be duplicated by the purchaser
for use in the purchaser's own classroom.

Copying any of these materials and distributing them
for any other purpose is a violation of the copyright laws.

© 2005 Teacher's Pet Publications, Inc.
www.tpet.com

INTRODUCTION
If you already own the LitPlan for this title, this Puzzle Pack will refresh your Unit Resource Materials and Vocabulary Resource Materials sections plus give you additional materials you can substitute into the tests. If you do not already have a complete LitPlan, these pages will give you some supplemental materials to use with your own plan. There are two main groups of materials: one set for unit words (such as characters' names, symbols, places, etc.) and one set for vocabulary words associated with the book.

WORD LIST
There is a word list for both the unit words and the vocabulary words. These lists show you which words are being used in the materials and the clues or definitions being used for those words. You may want to give students a word list with clues/definitions to help them, or you may want students to only have a word list (without clues/definitions) if you want them to work a little harder. Both are available for duplication. The word lists can also be your "calling key" for the bingo games.

FILL IN THE BLANK AND MATCHING
There are 4 each of the fill in the blank and matching worksheets for both the unit and vocabulary words. These pages can be used either as extra worksheets for students or as objective parts of a unit test. They can be done individually if students need extra help or as a whole class activity to review the material covered.

MAGIC SQUARES
The magic squares not only reinforce the material covered but also work on reasoning and math skills. Many teachers have told us that their students really enjoy doing these!

WORD SEARCH PUZZLES
The word search words go in all directions, as indicated on your answer keys. Two of the word search puzzles have the clues listed rather than the words. This makes the puzzle a little more difficult, but it reinforces the material better. Two word search puzzles have words only for students who find the clue puzzles too difficult.

CROSSWORD PUZZLES
Both unit and vocabulary word sections have 4 crossword puzzles.

BINGO CARDS
There are 32 individual bingo cards for the unit words and 32 individual bingo cards for the vocabulary words. You can use your word list as a "call list," calling the words at random and marking them off of your list as you go, or you could use the flash cards by cutting them apart and drawing the words at random from a hat (or box or whatever). To make a better review, you might ask for the definition and spelling of each word as you call it out–or you could call out the definitions and have students tell you the words they need to look for on the puzzle.

JUGGLE LETTERS
The vocabulary juggle letter game is intended to help students learn the spellings of the words. One sheet has the definitions listed on it as an extra help for students who need it or to reinforce the definitions if you choose to do so.

FLASH CARDS
We've included a set of vocabulary flash cards you can duplicate, cut, and fold for your students. Some teachers make a few sets for general use by the class; others make a set for each student. Some teachers duplicate them for each student and have the students cut & fold their own. You can cut out just the words and put them in a hat, have each student pick out one word and write the definition and a sentence for that word. Students then swap words and papers, with the next student adding a sentence of his own under the last one. You can have students swap as many times as you like. Each time the student will read the sentences written prior to his own and then add a sentence. You can cut out the words and definitions separately and play "I Have; Who Has?" Each student in the room draws a word and definition. The first student says, "I have (the name of the word). Who has the definition?" The student with the definition reads it then says, "I have (the name of the vocabulary word she has). Who has the definition?" The round continues until all words and definitions have been given.

The Hobbit Word List

No.	Word	Clue/Definition
1.	ARKENSTONE	Greatest single treasure
2.	AZOG	Goblin that killed Thorin's grandfather
3.	BARD	Killed Smaug with a black arrow
4.	BARRELS	Escape vehicles to take dwarves away from woodelves
5.	BEORN	Bear-man
6.	BILBO	Mr. Baggins
7.	BITER	___ & Beater; goblin names for Orcrist & Glamdring
8.	BLACK	____ River; river in Mirkwood
9.	BOAT	Used to cross the black water
10.	BOMBUR	Got wet in the enchanted black water
11.	CRAM	Biscuit-like food
12.	CUP	Bilbo took this item, which made Smaug angry
13.	DAIN	Leader of the dwarves after Thorin
14.	DALE	Town ruins in the shadow of the mountain
15.	DURIN	Elf New Year; ___'s Day
16.	DWARF	Dwalin, Bifur or Dori, for example
17.	EAGLES	Saved Thorin & Co. from the wargs & goblins
18.	ELROND	King of the Elves
19.	ELVES	Dwarves thought these creatures were foolish
20.	ESGAROTH	Lake town
21.	FIVE	Battle of ____ Armies
22.	GANDALF	Wizard
23.	GLAMDRING	The Foe Hammer
24.	GOBLIN	Azog, for example
25.	GOLLUM	Pale-eyed water creature
26.	GREEN	_____ Dragon Inn
27.	HOBBIT	Bilbo, for example
28.	HOMELY	Last ____ Home; Elrond's home
29.	KEY	It opened the secret door in the mountain
30.	KING	Elrond was ___ of the Elves
31.	LIGHTS	Travelers left the path to see what was at these
32.	LONE	____ Lands; where Bilbo first wished he were home
33.	LONELY	___ Mountain; where Smaug lived
34.	MAP	Gandalf gave Thorin this and a key
35.	MIRKWOOD	Never leave the path in this place
36.	MISTY	_____ Mountains
37.	MOUNTAIN	Misty or Lonely
38.	NECKLACE	Bilbo's gift to Elvenking to repay his hospitality
39.	NECROMANCER	Council of Wizards drove the ____ out of southern Mirkwood
40.	ORCRIST	The Goblin Cleaver
41.	PATH	Never leave the ___ in Mirkwood
42.	PINECONES	Gandalf lit them on fire & threw them at wargs
43.	PIPE	Bilbo's smoking device
44.	POCKETS	Gollum couldn't guess what was in Bilbo's ___
45.	PONIES	Beorn loaned these as transportation for the travelers
46.	RAVENHILL	Old watch post on SW side of mountain
47.	RIDDLES	Bilbo & Gollum's game
48.	RING	Gollum's birthday present that Bilbo found
49.	RIVENDELL	Land of the elves
50.	ROAC	Raven; son of Carc
51.	SECRET	Travelers looked for the ___ entrance to the mountain

The Hobbit Word List Continued

No.	Word	Clue/Definition
52.	SHADOW	Bilbo's showed even when he wore the ring
53.	SMAUG	Dragon
54.	SMELL	Smaug's sense of ___ was keen
55.	SMOKE	Smaug's puff
56.	SPIDERS	Killing one gave Bilbo confidence
57.	STING	Bilbo's name for his knife
58.	STONE	Trolls turned to ___ in the sun
59.	SWORDS	Gandalf and Thorin took ___ from the trolls' cave
60.	THORIN	His grandfather was King of the Mountain
61.	THRUSHES	Tame messenger birds
62.	TOLKIEN	Author
63.	TOOK	The ____ in Bilbo made him adventurous
64.	TREASURE	Smaug slept on it
65.	TREES	Thorin & Co. climbed in them to avoid wargs
66.	TROLL	Bert or Tom, for example
67.	WARGS	Evil wolves
68.	WILLIAM	Troll who caught Bilbo trying to pick his pocket
69.	WOODELVES	Captured the dwarves & actually saved them

The Hobbit Fill In The Blanks 1

_____   1. Gollum's birthday present that Bilbo found
_____   2. ____ Lands; where Bilbo first wished he were home
_____   3. Travelers looked for the ___ entrance to the mountain
_____   4. Bear-man
_____   5. Smaug slept on it
_____   6. Evil wolves
_____   7. The ____ in Bilbo made him adventurous
_____   8. Leader of the dwarves after Thorin
_____   9. ____ River; river in Mirkwood
_____   10. ____ Dragon Inn
_____   11. Escape vehicles to take dwarves away from woodelves
_____   12. Council of Wizards drove the ____ out of southern Mirkwood
_____   13. Town ruins in the shadow of the mountain
_____   14. Smaug's sense of ___ was keen
_____   15. Bilbo's name for his knife
_____   16. Travelers left the path to see what was at these
_____   17. Bilbo took this item, which made Smaug angry
_____   18. Bert or Tom, for example
_____   19. Battle of ____ Armies
_____   20. Saved Thorin & Co. from the wargs & goblins

The Hobbit Fill In The Blanks 1 Answer Key

Answer	Clue
RING	1. Gollum's birthday present that Bilbo found
LONE	2. ____ Lands; where Bilbo first wished he were home
SECRET	3. Travelers looked for the ___ entrance to the mountain
BEORN	4. Bear-man
TREASURE	5. Smaug slept on it
WARGS	6. Evil wolves
TOOK	7. The ____ in Bilbo made him adventurous
DAIN	8. Leader of the dwarves after Thorin
BLACK	9. ____ River; river in Mirkwood
GREEN	10. _____ Dragon Inn
BARRELS	11. Escape vehicles to take dwarves away from woodelves
NECROMANCER	12. Council of Wizards drove the ____ out of southern Mirkwood
DALE	13. Town ruins in the shadow of the mountain
SMELL	14. Smaug's sense of ___ was keen
STING	15. Bilbo's name for his knife
LIGHTS	16. Travelers left the path to see what was at these
CUP	17. Bilbo took this item, which made Smaug angry
TROLL	18. Bert or Tom, for example
FIVE	19. Battle of ____ Armies
EAGLES	20. Saved Thorin & Co. from the wargs & goblins

The Hobbit Fill In The Blanks 2

_____ 1. Wizard

_____ 2. Bilbo, for example

_____ 3. The Goblin Cleaver

_____ 4. Saved Thorin & Co. from the wargs & goblins

_____ 5. Escape vehicles to take dwarves away from woodelves

_____ 6. Old watch post on SW side of mountain

_____ 7. Biscuit-like food

_____ 8. Dwalin, Bifur or Dori, for example

_____ 9. Never leave the ___ in Mirkwood

_____ 10. Never leave the path in this place

_____ 11. ___ Mountain; where Smaug lived

_____ 12. Thorin & Co. climbed in them to avoid wargs

_____ 13. Lake town

_____ 14. ____ River; river in Mirkwood

_____ 15. _____ Dragon Inn

_____ 16. Troll who caught Bilbo trying to pick his pocket

_____ 17. Raven; son of Carc

_____ 18. Dwarves thought these creatures were foolish

_____ 19. Elf New Year; ___'s Day

_____ 20. King of the Elves

The Hobbit Fill In The Blanks 2 Answer Key

GANDALF	1. Wizard
HOBBIT	2. Bilbo, for example
ORCRIST	3. The Goblin Cleaver
EAGLES	4. Saved Thorin & Co. from the wargs & goblins
BARRELS	5. Escape vehicles to take dwarves away from woodelves
RAVENHILL	6. Old watch post on SW side of mountain
CRAM	7. Biscuit-like food
DWARF	8. Dwalin, Bifur or Dori, for example
PATH	9. Never leave the ___ in Mirkwood
MIRKWOOD	10. Never leave the path in this place
LONELY	11. ___ Mountain; where Smaug lived
TREES	12. Thorin & Co. climbed in them to avoid wargs
ESGAROTH	13. Lake town
BLACK	14. ____ River; river in Mirkwood
GREEN	15. _____ Dragon Inn
WILLIAM	16. Troll who caught Bilbo trying to pick his pocket
ROAC	17. Raven; son of Carc
ELVES	18. Dwarves thought these creatures were foolish
DURIN	19. Elf New Year; ___'s Day
ELROND	20. King of the Elves

The Hobbit Fill In The Blanks 3

_____ 1. Author
_____ 2. It opened the secret door in the mountain
_____ 3. Gollum couldn't guess what was in Bilbo's ___
_____ 4. Mr. Baggins
_____ 5. Bilbo & Gollum's game
_____ 6. Bilbo took this item, which made Smaug angry
_____ 7. Thorin & Co. climbed in them to avoid wargs
_____ 8. Bilbo's name for his knife
_____ 9. Town ruins in the shadow of the mountain
_____ 10. Biscuit-like food
_____ 11. Never leave the ___ in Mirkwood
_____ 12. Gandalf gave Thorin this and a key
_____ 13. Troll who caught Bilbo trying to pick his pocket
_____ 14. Tame messenger birds
_____ 15. Council of Wizards drove the ____ out of southern Mirkwood
_____ 16. Dwalin, Bifur or Dori, for example
_____ 17. Old watch post on SW side of mountain
_____ 18. Wizard
_____ 19. Got wet in the enchanted black water
_____ 20. Battle of ____ Armies

The Hobbit Fill In The Blanks 3 Answer Key

Answer	Clue
TOLKIEN	1. Author
KEY	2. It opened the secret door in the mountain
POCKETS	3. Gollum couldn't guess what was in Bilbo's ___
BILBO	4. Mr. Baggins
RIDDLES	5. Bilbo & Gollum's game
CUP	6. Bilbo took this item, which made Smaug angry
TREES	7. Thorin & Co. climbed in them to avoid wargs
STING	8. Bilbo's name for his knife
DALE	9. Town ruins in the shadow of the mountain
CRAM	10. Biscuit-like food
PATH	11. Never leave the ___ in Mirkwood
MAP	12. Gandalf gave Thorin this and a key
WILLIAM	13. Troll who caught Bilbo trying to pick his pocket
THRUSHES	14. Tame messenger birds
NECROMANCER	15. Council of Wizards drove the ___ out of southern Mirkwood
DWARF	16. Dwalin, Bifur or Dori, for example
RAVENHILL	17. Old watch post on SW side of mountain
GANDALF	18. Wizard
BOMBUR	19. Got wet in the enchanted black water
FIVE	20. Battle of ___ Armies

The Hobbit Fill In The Blanks 4

_____ 1. Troll who caught Bilbo trying to pick his pocket

_____ 2. His grandfather was King of the Mountain

_____ 3. _____ Dragon Inn

_____ 4. Bilbo & Gollum's game

_____ 5. Bilbo, for example

_____ 6. Bilbo's name for his knife

_____ 7. Bilbo's smoking device

_____ 8. Saved Thorin & Co. from the wargs & goblins

_____ 9. Thorin & Co. climbed in them to avoid wargs

_____ 10. Pale-eyed water creature

_____ 11. Leader of the dwarves after Thorin

_____ 12. Killing one gave Bilbo confidence

_____ 13. Dragon

_____ 14. Killed Smaug with a black arrow

_____ 15. Biscuit-like food

_____ 16. Dwarves thought these creatures were foolish

_____ 17. Land of the elves

_____ 18. Mr. Baggins

_____ 19. Misty or Lonely

_____ 20. Beorn loaned these as transportation for the travelers

The Hobbit Fill In The Blanks 4 Answer Key

WILLIAM	1. Troll who caught Bilbo trying to pick his pocket
THORIN	2. His grandfather was King of the Mountain
GREEN	3. _____ Dragon Inn
RIDDLES	4. Bilbo & Gollum's game
HOBBIT	5. Bilbo, for example
STING	6. Bilbo's name for his knife
PIPE	7. Bilbo's smoking device
EAGLES	8. Saved Thorin & Co. from the wargs & goblins
TREES	9. Thorin & Co. climbed in them to avoid wargs
GOLLUM	10. Pale-eyed water creature
DAIN	11. Leader of the dwarves after Thorin
SPIDERS	12. Killing one gave Bilbo confidence
SMAUG	13. Dragon
BARD	14. Killed Smaug with a black arrow
CRAM	15. Biscuit-like food
ELVES	16. Dwarves thought these creatures were foolish
RIVENDELL	17. Land of the elves
BILBO	18. Mr. Baggins
MOUNTAIN	19. Misty or Lonely
PONIES	20. Beorn loaned these as transportation for the travelers

The Hobbit Matching 1

___ 1. HOMELY   A. Travelers left the path to see what was at these
___ 2. MIRKWOOD   B. Elrond was ___ of the Elves
___ 3. MAP   C. Gandalf gave Thorin this and a key
___ 4. LONELY   D. Saved Thorin & Co. from the wargs & goblins
___ 5. LIGHTS   E. Captured the dwarves & actually saved them
___ 6. KING   F. Biscuit-like food
___ 7. MOUNTAIN   G. Author
___ 8. SMOKE   H. Battle of ___ Armies
___ 9. PINECONES   I. ___ Mountains
___10. RIDDLES   J. Gollum's birthday present that Bilbo found
___11. WOODELVES   K. Smaug's puff
___12. FIVE   L. ___ Mountain; where Smaug lived
___13. MISTY   M. Bilbo's gift to Elvenking to repay his hospitality
___14. NECKLACE   N. Never leave the path in this place
___15. TROLL   O. Lake town
___16. RAVENHILL   P. Bert or Tom, for example
___17. ELVES   Q. Gandalf lit them on fire & threw them at wargs
___18. EAGLES   R. Last ___ Home; Elrond's home
___19. DWARF   S. Old watch post on SW side of mountain
___20. GANDALF   T. Wizard
___21. BOAT   U. Used to cross the black water
___22. CRAM   V. Dwalin, Bifur or Dori, for example
___23. TOLKIEN   W. Misty or Lonely
___24. ESGAROTH   X. Dwarves thought these creatures were foolish
___25. RING   Y. Bilbo & Gollum's game

The Hobbit Matching 1 Answer Key

R - 1. HOMELY	A. Travelers left the path to see what was at these
N - 2. MIRKWOOD	B. Elrond was ___ of the Elves
C - 3. MAP	C. Gandalf gave Thorin this and a key
L - 4. LONELY	D. Saved Thorin & Co. from the wargs & goblins
A - 5. LIGHTS	E. Captured the dwarves & actually saved them
B - 6. KING	F. Biscuit-like food
W - 7. MOUNTAIN	G. Author
K - 8. SMOKE	H. Battle of ___ Armies
Q - 9. PINECONES	I. ___ Mountains
Y - 10. RIDDLES	J. Gollum's birthday present that Bilbo found
E - 11. WOODELVES	K. Smaug's puff
H - 12. FIVE	L. ___ Mountain; where Smaug lived
I - 13. MISTY	M. Bilbo's gift to Elvenking to repay his hospitality
M - 14. NECKLACE	N. Never leave the path in this place
P - 15. TROLL	O. Lake town
S - 16. RAVENHILL	P. Bert or Tom, for example
X - 17. ELVES	Q. Gandalf lit them on fire & threw them at wargs
D - 18. EAGLES	R. Last ___ Home; Elrond's home
V - 19. DWARF	S. Old watch post on SW side of mountain
T - 20. GANDALF	T. Wizard
U - 21. BOAT	U. Used to cross the black water
F - 22. CRAM	V. Dwalin, Bifur or Dori, for example
G - 23. TOLKIEN	W. Misty or Lonely
O - 24. ESGAROTH	X. Dwarves thought these creatures were foolish
J - 25. RING	Y. Bilbo & Gollum's game

The Hobbit Matching 2

___ 1. BARRELS   A. _____ Dragon Inn
___ 2. DWARF   B. Bert or Tom, for example
___ 3. WILLIAM   C. ____ River; river in Mirkwood
___ 4. SPIDERS   D. Greatest single treasure
___ 5. DAIN   E. It opened the secret door in the mountain
___ 6. ARKENSTONE   F. Lake town
___ 7. CRAM   G. Escape vehicles to take dwarves away from woodelves
___ 8. ROAC   H. Leader of the dwarves after Thorin
___ 9. GREEN   I. The ____ in Bilbo made him adventurous
___10. PIPE   J. Trolls turned to ___ in the sun
___11. HOMELY   K. Gollum's birthday present that Bilbo found
___12. STONE   L. The Goblin Cleaver
___13. TOOK   M. Last ____ Home; Elrond's home
___14. TREASURE   N. Travelers left the path to see what was at these
___15. KEY   O. Killing one gave Bilbo confidence
___16. FIVE   P. Wizard
___17. RING   Q. Bilbo's smoking device
___18. STING   R. Bilbo's name for his knife
___19. BLACK   S. Biscuit-like food
___20. SMAUG   T. Battle of ____ Armies
___21. GANDALF   U. Smaug slept on it
___22. LIGHTS   V. Dwalin, Bifur or Dori, for example
___23. ORCRIST   W. Troll who caught Bilbo trying to pick his pocket
___24. TROLL   X. Dragon
___25. ESGAROTH   Y. Raven; son of Carc

The Hobbit Matching 2 Answer Key

G - 1. BARRELS	A.	_____ Dragon Inn
V - 2. DWARF	B.	Bert or Tom, for example
W - 3. WILLIAM	C.	_____ River; river in Mirkwood
O - 4. SPIDERS	D.	Greatest single treasure
H - 5. DAIN	E.	It opened the secret door in the mountain
D - 6. ARKENSTONE	F.	Lake town
S - 7. CRAM	G.	Escape vehicles to take dwarves away from woodelves
Y - 8. ROAC	H.	Leader of the dwarves after Thorin
A - 9. GREEN	I.	The _____ in Bilbo made him adventurous
Q - 10. PIPE	J.	Trolls turned to _____ in the sun
M - 11. HOMELY	K.	Gollum's birthday present that Bilbo found
J - 12. STONE	L.	The Goblin Cleaver
I - 13. TOOK	M.	Last _____ Home; Elrond's home
U - 14. TREASURE	N.	Travelers left the path to see what was at these
E - 15. KEY	O.	Killing one gave Bilbo confidence
T - 16. FIVE	P.	Wizard
K - 17. RING	Q.	Bilbo's smoking device
R - 18. STING	R.	Bilbo's name for his knife
C - 19. BLACK	S.	Biscuit-like food
X - 20. SMAUG	T.	Battle of _____ Armies
P - 21. GANDALF	U.	Smaug slept on it
N - 22. LIGHTS	V.	Dwalin, Bifur or Dori, for example
L - 23. ORCRIST	W.	Troll who caught Bilbo trying to pick his pocket
B - 24. TROLL	X.	Dragon
F - 25. ESGAROTH	Y.	Raven; son of Carc

The Hobbit Matching 3

___ 1. AZOG   A. Thorin & Co. climbed in them to avoid wargs
___ 2. CRAM   B. Used to cross the black water
___ 3. PIPE   C. Last ____ Home; Elrond's home
___ 4. RIDDLES   D. Gollum's birthday present that Bilbo found
___ 5. SMAUG   E. ___ Mountain; where Smaug lived
___ 6. ELROND   F. King of the Elves
___ 7. SMELL   G. Goblin that killed Thorin's grandfather
___ 8. BILBO   H. Smaug's sense of ___ was keen
___ 9. ELVES   I. Wizard
___ 10. TREES   J. Gollum couldn't guess what was in Bilbo's ___
___ 11. RING   K. Greatest single treasure
___ 12. FIVE   L. Killing one gave Bilbo confidence
___ 13. GANDALF   M. Raven; son of Carc
___ 14. STONE   N. Smaug slept on it
___ 15. ARKENSTONE   O. Dragon
___ 16. ROAC   P. Mr. Baggins
___ 17. LONELY   Q. Bilbo's name for his knife
___ 18. POCKETS   R. Bilbo & Gollum's game
___ 19. TREASURE   S. ____ River; river in Mirkwood
___ 20. TROLL   T. Dwarves thought these creatures were foolish
___ 21. BLACK   U. Bert or Tom, for example
___ 22. HOMELY   V. Biscuit-like food
___ 23. BOAT   W. Bilbo's smoking device
___ 24. SPIDERS   X. Battle of ____ Armies
___ 25. STING   Y. Trolls turned to ___ in the sun

The Hobbit Matching 3 Answer Key

G - 1. AZOG
V - 2. CRAM
W - 3. PIPE
R - 4. RIDDLES
O - 5. SMAUG
F - 6. ELROND
H - 7. SMELL
P - 8. BILBO
T - 9. ELVES
A - 10. TREES
D - 11. RING
X - 12. FIVE
I - 13. GANDALF
Y - 14. STONE
K - 15. ARKENSTONE
M - 16. ROAC
E - 17. LONELY
J - 18. POCKETS
N - 19. TREASURE
U - 20. TROLL
S - 21. BLACK
C - 22. HOMELY
B - 23. BOAT
L - 24. SPIDERS
Q - 25. STING

A. Thorin & Co. climbed in them to avoid wargs
B. Used to cross the black water
C. Last ____ Home; Elrond's home
D. Gollum's birthday present that Bilbo found
E. ____ Mountain; where Smaug lived
F. King of the Elves
G. Goblin that killed Thorin's grandfather
H. Smaug's sense of ____ was keen
I. Wizard
J. Gollum couldn't guess what was in Bilbo's ____
K. Greatest single treasure
L. Killing one gave Bilbo confidence
M. Raven; son of Carc
N. Smaug slept on it
O. Dragon
P. Mr. Baggins
Q. Bilbo's name for his knife
R. Bilbo & Gollum's game
S. ____ River; river in Mirkwood
T. Dwarves thought these creatures were foolish
U. Bert or Tom, for example
V. Biscuit-like food
W. Bilbo's smoking device
X. Battle of ____ Armies
Y. Trolls turned to ____ in the sun

The Hobbit Matching 4

___ 1. DURIN
___ 2. DAIN
___ 3. SECRET
___ 4. THORIN
___ 5. NECKLACE
___ 6. NECROMANCER
___ 7. CRAM
___ 8. BITER
___ 9. LONE
___ 10. STING
___ 11. GLAMDRING
___ 12. AZOG
___ 13. RAVENHILL
___ 14. MIRKWOOD
___ 15. BARRELS
___ 16. SPIDERS
___ 17. CUP
___ 18. ELROND
___ 19. WARGS
___ 20. LIGHTS
___ 21. GOLLUM
___ 22. PIPE
___ 23. WILLIAM
___ 24. SWORDS
___ 25. TROLL

A. Bert or Tom, for example
B. Troll who caught Bilbo trying to pick his pocket
C. His grandfather was King of the Mountain
D. Travelers left the path to see what was at these
E. Goblin that killed Thorin's grandfather
F. Gandalf and Thorin took ___ from the trolls' cave
G. Council of Wizards drove the ____ out of southern Mirkwood
H. ____ Lands; where Bilbo first wished he were home
I. Escape vehicles to take dwarves away from woodelves
J. Old watch post on SW side of mountain
K. Bilbo's name for his knife
L. Travelers looked for the ___ entrance to the mountain
M. Bilbo's gift to Elvenking to repay his hospitality
N. Biscuit-like food
O. ___ & Beater; goblin names for Orcrist & Glamdring
P. Pale-eyed water creature
Q. Leader of the dwarves after Thorin
R. Bilbo took this item, which made Smaug angry
S. King of the Elves
T. Elf New Year; ___'s Day
U. Killing one gave Bilbo confidence
V. Evil wolves
W. Bilbo's smoking device
X. The Foe Hammer
Y. Never leave the path in this place

The Hobbit Matching 4 Answer Key

T - 1. DURIN	A.	Bert or Tom, for example
Q - 2. DAIN	B.	Troll who caught Bilbo trying to pick his pocket
L - 3. SECRET	C.	His grandfather was King of the Mountain
C - 4. THORIN	D.	Travelers left the path to see what was at these
M - 5. NECKLACE	E.	Goblin that killed Thorin's grandfather
G - 6. NECROMANCER	F.	Gandalf and Thorin took ___ from the trolls' cave
N - 7. CRAM	G.	Council of Wizards drove the ___ out of southern Mirkwood
O - 8. BITER	H.	___ Lands; where Bilbo first wished he were home
H - 9. LONE	I.	Escape vehicles to take dwarves away from woodelves
K - 10. STING	J.	Old watch post on SW side of mountain
X - 11. GLAMDRING	K.	Bilbo's name for his knife
E - 12. AZOG	L.	Travelers looked for the ___ entrance to the mountain
J - 13. RAVENHILL	M.	Bilbo's gift to Elvenking to repay his hospitality
Y - 14. MIRKWOOD	N.	Biscuit-like food
I - 15. BARRELS	O.	___ & Beater; goblin names for Orcrist & Glamdring
U - 16. SPIDERS	P.	Pale-eyed water creature
R - 17. CUP	Q.	Leader of the dwarves after Thorin
S - 18. ELROND	R.	Bilbo took this item, which made Smaug angry
V - 19. WARGS	S.	King of the Elves
D - 20. LIGHTS	T.	Elf New Year; ___'s Day
P - 21. GOLLUM	U.	Killing one gave Bilbo confidence
W - 22. PIPE	V.	Evil wolves
B - 23. WILLIAM	W.	Bilbo's smoking device
F - 24. SWORDS	X.	The Foe Hammer
A - 25. TROLL	Y.	Never leave the path in this place

The Hobbit Magic Squares 1

Match the definition with the vocabulary word. Put your answers in the magic squares below. When your answers are correct, all columns and rows will add to the same number.

A. KING
B. MIRKWOOD
C. BOAT
D. GANDALF
E. ESGAROTH
F. WILLIAM
G. WOODELVES
H. ARKENSTONE
I. AZOG
J. RIVENDELL
K. STING
L. DALE
M. SWORDS
N. SMAUG
O. MOUNTAIN
P. NECROMANCER

1. Never leave the path in this place
2. Captured the dwarves & actually saved them
3. Bilbo's name for his knife
4. Dragon
5. Gandalf and Thorin took ___ from the trolls' cave
6. Town ruins in the shadow of the mountain
7. Greatest single treasure
8. Elrond was ___ of the Elves
9. Council of Wizards drove the ____ out of southern Mirkwood
10. Goblin that killed Thorin's grandfather
11. Lake town
12. Wizard
13. Used to cross the black water
14. Troll who caught Bilbo trying to pick his pocket
15. Land of the elves
16. Misty or Lonely

A=	B=	C=	D=
E=	F=	G=	H=
I=	J=	K=	L=
M=	N=	O=	P=

The Hobbit Magic Squares 1 Answer Key

Match the definition with the vocabulary word. Put your answers in the magic squares below. When your answers are correct, all columns and rows will add to the same number.

A. KING
B. MIRKWOOD
C. BOAT
D. GANDALF
E. ESGAROTH
F. WILLIAM
G. WOODELVES
H. ARKENSTONE
I. AZOG
J. RIVENDELL
K. STING
L. DALE
M. SWORDS
N. SMAUG
O. MOUNTAIN
P. NECROMANCER

1. Never leave the path in this place
2. Captured the dwarves & actually saved them
3. Bilbo's name for his knife
4. Dragon
5. Gandalf and Thorin took ___ from the trolls' cave
6. Town ruins in the shadow of the mountain
7. Greatest single treasure
8. Elrond was ___ of the Elves
9. Council of Wizards drove the ____ out of southern Mirkwood
10. Goblin that killed Thorin's grandfather
11. Lake town
12. Wizard
13. Used to cross the black water
14. Troll who caught Bilbo trying to pick his pocket
15. Land of the elves
16. Misty or Lonely

A=8	B=1	C=13	D=12
E=11	F=14	G=2	H=7
I=10	J=15	K=3	L=6
M=5	N=4	O=16	P=9

The Hobbit Magic Squares 2

Match the definition with the vocabulary word. Put your answers in the magic squares below. When your answers are correct, all columns and rows will add to the same number.

A. TREASURE
B. BARD
C. SMOKE
D. THORIN
E. THRUSHES
F. BARRELS
G. DWARF
H. SHADOW
I. EAGLES
J. MIRKWOOD
K. WOODELVES
L. KEY
M. SMELL
N. TREES
O. TOLKIEN
P. LIGHTS

1. Escape vehicles to take dwarves away from woodelves
2. Saved Thorin & Co. from the wargs & goblins
3. Author
4. His grandfather was King of the Mountain
5. Smaug's sense of ___ was keen
6. Killed Smaug with a black arrow
7. Bilbo's showed even when he wore the ring
8. Captured the dwarves & actually saved them
9. Smaug's puff
10. Travelers left the path to see what was at these
11. Never leave the path in this place
12. Tame messenger birds
13. It opened the secret door in the mountain
14. Dwalin, Bifur or Dori, for example
15. Smaug slept on it
16. Thorin & Co. climbed in them to avoid wargs

A=	B=	C=	D=
E=	F=	G=	H=
I=	J=	K=	L=
M=	N=	O=	P=

The Hobbit Magic Squares 2 Answer Key

Match the definition with the vocabulary word. Put your answers in the magic squares below. When your answers are correct, all columns and rows will add to the same number.

A. TREASURE
B. BARD
C. SMOKE
D. THORIN
E. THRUSHES
F. BARRELS
G. DWARF
H. SHADOW
I. EAGLES
J. MIRKWOOD
K. WOODELVES
L. KEY
M. SMELL
N. TREES
O. TOLKIEN
P. LIGHTS

1. Escape vehicles to take dwarves away from woodelves
2. Saved Thorin & Co. from the wargs & goblins
3. Author
4. His grandfather was King of the Mountain
5. Smaug's sense of ___ was keen
6. Killed Smaug with a black arrow
7. Bilbo's showed even when he wore the ring
8. Captured the dwarves & actually saved them
9. Smaug's puff
10. Travelers left the path to see what was at these
11. Never leave the path in this place
12. Tame messenger birds
13. It opened the secret door in the mountain
14. Dwalin, Bifur or Dori, for example
15. Smaug slept on it
16. Thorin & Co. climbed in them to avoid wargs

A=15	B=6	C=9	D=4
E=12	F=1	G=14	H=7
I=2	J=11	K=8	L=13
M=5	N=16	O=3	P=10

The Hobbit Magic Squares 3

Match the definition with the vocabulary word. Put your answers in the magic squares below. When your answers are correct, all columns and rows will add to the same number.

A. LONE
B. PONIES
C. BLACK
D. BEORN
E. GANDALF
F. WARGS
G. TREASURE
H. WOODELVES
I. SPIDERS
J. SMELL
K. THORIN
L. NECKLACE
M. RING
N. STONE
O. TROLL
P. PIPE

1. Gollum's birthday present that Bilbo found
2. Evil wolves
3. Captured the dwarves & actually saved them
4. Bert or Tom, for example
5. Bilbo's gift to Elvenking to repay his hospitality
6. ____ River; river in Mirkwood
7. ____ Lands; where Bilbo first wished he were home
8. Smaug's sense of ___ was keen
9. His grandfather was King of the Mountain
10. Bear-man
11. Beorn loaned these as transportation for the travelers
12. Killing one gave Bilbo confidence
13. Trolls turned to ___ in the sun
14. Wizard
15. Smaug slept on it
16. Bilbo's smoking device

A=	B=	C=	D=
E=	F=	G=	H=
I=	J=	K=	L=
M=	N=	O=	P=

The Hobbit Magic Squares 3 Answer Key

Match the definition with the vocabulary word. Put your answers in the magic squares below. When your answers are correct, all columns and rows will add to the same number.

A. LONE
B. PONIES
C. BLACK
D. BEORN
E. GANDALF
F. WARGS
G. TREASURE
H. WOODELVES
I. SPIDERS
J. SMELL
K. THORIN
L. NECKLACE
M. RING
N. STONE
O. TROLL
P. PIPE

1. Gollum's birthday present that Bilbo found
2. Evil wolves
3. Captured the dwarves & actually saved them
4. Bert or Tom, for example
5. Bilbo's gift to Elvenking to repay his hospitality
6. ____ River; river in Mirkwood
7. ____ Lands; where Bilbo first wished he were home
8. Smaug's sense of ___ was keen
9. His grandfather was King of the Mountain
10. Bear-man
11. Beorn loaned these as transportation for the travelers
12. Killing one gave Bilbo confidence
13. Trolls turned to ___ in the sun
14. Wizard
15. Smaug slept on it
16. Bilbo's smoking device

A=7	B=11	C=6	D=10
E=14	F=2	G=15	H=3
I=12	J=8	K=9	L=5
M=1	N=13	O=4	P=16

The Hobbit Magic Squares 4

Match the definition with the vocabulary word. Put your answers in the magic squares below. When your answers are correct, all columns and rows will add to the same number.

A. SMAUG
B. WARGS
C. DURIN
D. ESGAROTH
E. THORIN
F. STONE
G. SWORDS
H. NECKLACE
I. BOAT
J. RIVENDELL
K. BARD
L. SECRET
M. TROLL
N. ARKENSTONE
O. WILLIAM
P. MIRKWOOD

1. Dragon
2. Greatest single treasure
3. Land of the elves
4. His grandfather was King of the Mountain
5. Gandalf and Thorin took ___ from the trolls' cave
6. Travelers looked for the ___ entrance to the mountain
7. Never leave the path in this place
8. Elf New Year; ___'s Day
9. Troll who caught Bilbo trying to pick his pocket
10. Lake town
11. Bilbo's gift to Elvenking to repay his hospitality
12. Killed Smaug with a black arrow
13. Used to cross the black water
14. Trolls turned to ___ in the sun
15. Evil wolves
16. Bert or Tom, for example

A=	B=	C=	D=
E=	F=	G=	H=
I=	J=	K=	L=
M=	N=	O=	P=

The Hobbit Magic Squares 4 Answer Key

Match the definition with the vocabulary word. Put your answers in the magic squares below. When your answers are correct, all columns and rows will add to the same number.

A. SMAUG
B. WARGS
C. DURIN
D. ESGAROTH
E. THORIN
F. STONE
G. SWORDS
H. NECKLACE
I. BOAT
J. RIVENDELL
K. BARD
L. SECRET
M. TROLL
N. ARKENSTONE
O. WILLIAM
P. MIRKWOOD

1. Dragon
2. Greatest single treasure
3. Land of the elves
4. His grandfather was King of the Mountain
5. Gandalf and Thorin took ___ from the trolls' cave
6. Travelers looked for the ___ entrance to the mountain
7. Never leave the path in this place
8. Elf New Year; ___'s Day
9. Troll who caught Bilbo trying to pick his pocket
10. Lake town
11. Bilbo's gift to Elvenking to repay his hospitality
12. Killed Smaug with a black arrow
13. Used to cross the black water
14. Trolls turned to ___ in the sun
15. Evil wolves
16. Bert or Tom, for example

A=1	B=15	C=8	D=10
E=4	F=14	G=5	H=11
I=13	J=3	K=12	L=6
M=16	N=2	O=9	P=7

The Hobbit Word Search 1

```
X R F E G R E E N B A R D K S K H P B H
V K V S P F N I I H Y O I T T E O O N
W A R G S O A N R H T A P N H Y B N A X
R Q M A L D N E U Z B C V R G L B I T Q
D W A R F Q Y C D M I S T Y I G I E S J
N N N O R S D R O W S P T B L D T S M N
O D R T I N S O D G N I K I M R D L O S
R W W H V T H M M B S D S Q N A R L K S
L D A L E S H A D O W E J J P G P I E K
E H F K N E R N C J E R C U P T R H R S
X M C N D C W C D R J S C R S T S N U J
G O S J E A S E T F I V E I E U A E S G
P S M E L L E R H B E O R N R T Z V A K
T R O L L K L P O W R C S H S O O A E C
S M A U G C G I R R E T I B O G R R X
V S E V L E A P I O K B L A C K N J T Y
P S S T O N E E N X L T O L K I E N Y W
```

Author (7)
Battle of ____ Armies (4)
Bear-man (5)
Beorn loaned these as transportation for the travelers (6)
Bert or Tom, for example (5)
Bilbo & Gollum's game (7)
Bilbo took this item, which made Smaug angry (3)
Bilbo's gift to Elvenking to repay his hospitality (8)
Bilbo's name for his knife (5)
Bilbo's showed even when he wore the ring (6)
Bilbo's smoking device (4)
Bilbo, for example (6)
Biscuit-like food (4)
Council of Wizards drove the ____ out of southern Mirkwood (11)
Dragon (5)
Dwalin, Bifur or Dori, for example (5)
Dwarves thought these creatures were foolish (5)
Elf New Year; ___'s Day (5)
Elrond was ___ of the Elves (4)
Evil wolves (5)
Gandalf and Thorin took ___ from the trolls' cave (6)
Gandalf gave Thorin this and a key (3)
Goblin that killed Thorin's grandfather (4)
Gollum couldn't guess what was in Bilbo's ___ (7)
Gollum's birthday present that Bilbo found (4)
His grandfather was King of the Mountain (6)
It opened the secret door in the mountain (3)
Killed Smaug with a black arrow (4)

Killing one gave Bilbo confidence (7)
King of the Elves (6)
Lake town (8)
Land of the elves (9)
Leader of the dwarves after Thorin (4)
Mr. Baggins (5)
Never leave the ___ in Mirkwood (4)
Old watch post on SW side of mountain (9)
Raven; son of Carc (4)
Saved Thorin & Co. from the wargs & goblins (6)
Smaug slept on it (8)
Smaug's puff (5)
Smaug's sense of ___ was keen (5)
Tame messenger birds (8)
The Goblin Cleaver (7)
The ____ in Bilbo made him adventurous (4)
Thorin & Co. climbed in them to avoid wargs (5)
Town ruins in the shadow of the mountain (4)
Travelers left the path to see what was at these (6)
Travelers looked for the ___ entrance to the mountain (6)
Trolls turned to ___ in the sun (5)
Used to cross the black water (4)
___ & Beater; goblin names for Orcrist & Glamdring (5)
____ Lands; where Bilbo first wished he were home (4)
____ River; river in Mirkwood (5)
_____ Dragon Inn (5)
_____ Mountains (5)

The Hobbit Word Search 1 Answer Key

```
        E   G R E E N B A R D     S K H P B
        S       N   I         O     T E O O O
W A R G S O A N R H T A P N H Y B N A
      A   L   D   E   U     C   R G L B I T
D W A R F         C D M I S T Y I   I E S
N         O R S D R O W S P T B L D T S M
O         T I     S O   G N I K I M   D L O
R         H V T     M M   S D S   N A   L K S
L   D A L E S H A D O W E   R C U   T   I R
E       K N E R N       E   S C R S   S N U S
    C     D C   C     R   S C R S   S N U
    O     E A S E T F I V E I E U A E S
P S M E L L E R H B E O R N R T Z V A
T R O L L K L P O       C H     O O A E
S M A U G C G I R   R E T I B O G R R
  S E V L E A P I O   B L A C K     T
        S T O N E E N     T O L K I E N
```

Author (7)
Battle of ____ Armies (4)
Bear-man (5)
Beorn loaned these as transportation for the travelers (6)
Bert or Tom, for example (5)
Bilbo & Gollum's game (7)
Bilbo took this item, which made Smaug angry (3)
Bilbo's gift to Elvenking to repay his hospitality (8)
Bilbo's name for his knife (5)
Bilbo's showed even when he wore the ring (6)
Bilbo's smoking device (4)
Bilbo, for example (6)
Biscuit-like food (4)
Council of Wizards drove the ____ out of southern Mirkwood (11)
Dragon (5)
Dwalin, Bifur or Dori, for example (5)
Dwarves thought these creatures were foolish (5)
Elf New Year; ___'s Day (5)
Elrond was ___ of the Elves (4)
Evil wolves (5)
Gandalf and Thorin took ___ from the trolls' cave (6)
Gandalf gave Thorin this and a key (3)
Goblin that killed Thorin's grandfather (4)
Gollum couldn't guess what was in Bilbo's ___ (7)
Gollum's birthday present that Bilbo found (4)
His grandfather was King of the Mountain (6)
It opened the secret door in the mountain (3)
Killed Smaug with a black arrow (4)

Killing one gave Bilbo confidence (7)
King of the Elves (6)
Lake town (8)
Land of the elves (9)
Leader of the dwarves after Thorin (4)
Mr. Baggins (5)
Never leave the ___ in Mirkwood (4)
Old watch post on SW side of mountain (9)
Raven; son of Carc (4)
Saved Thorin & Co. from the wargs & goblins (6)
Smaug slept on it (8)
Smaug's puff (5)
Smaug's sense of ___ was keen (5)
Tame messenger birds (8)
The Goblin Cleaver (7)
The ____ in Bilbo made him adventurous (4)
Thorin & Co. climbed in them to avoid wargs (5)
Town ruins in the shadow of the mountain (4)
Travelers left the path to see what was at these (6)
Travelers looked for the ___ entrance to the mountain (6)
Trolls turned to ___ in the sun (5)
Used to cross the black water (4)
___ & Beater; goblin names for Orcrist & Glamdring (5)
____ Lands; where Bilbo first wished he were home (4)
____ River; river in Mirkwood (5)
_____ Dragon Inn (5)
_____ Mountains (5)

The Hobbit Word Search 2

```
R O A C S E H E B C D B B S N F K H D S
V T Z D M T S A S I A E W C I N X I D B
B O D M A P Y G B G L A M D R I N G N R
C O H P U I R L A V E B N R O A G N O G
G K A Z G A N E E R G B O A H Q M I R Q
S T W T W K S S R O I F B T E L T L C
B T R A V E N H I L L T S I K E Y S E X
L I O L V E O V A S Q E H O V D T E P T
A B J N E M E D T D H R M P R E Q C I W
C B G R E N G D N S O S M U K G J R P P
K O G L D G O R U L P W R C S Y Y E D C
G H Y E O O A R O R M U O T L T M T U T
O J L Z W W H N M P B P H E S K N F R K
L L A K C T E S D M H G N I N R R E I C
T R O L L V J O A I O M M O A E Y N S
U I S M E L L B R L L D X E W S K G B S
M P I N E C O N E S F F B D P O N I E S
```

Battle of ____ Armies (4)
Bear-man (5)
Beorn loaned these as transportation for the travelers (6)
Bert or Tom, for example (5)
Bilbo took this item, which made Smaug angry (3)
Bilbo's name for his knife (5)
Bilbo's showed even when he wore the ring (6)
Bilbo's smoking device (4)
Bilbo, for example (6)
Biscuit-like food (4)
Dragon (5)
Dwalin, Bifur or Dori, for example (5)
Dwarves thought these creatures were foolish (5)
Elf New Year; ___'s Day (5)
Elrond was ___ of the Elves (4)
Evil wolves (5)
Gandalf gave Thorin this and a key (3)
Gandalf lit them on fire & threw them at wargs (9)
Goblin that killed Thorin's grandfather (4)
Gollum couldn't guess what was in Bilbo's ___ (7)
Gollum's birthday present that Bilbo found (4)
Got wet in the enchanted black water (6)
His grandfather was King of the Mountain (6)
It opened the secret door in the mountain (3)
Killed Smaug with a black arrow (4)
King of the Elves (6)
Lake town (8)
Land of the elves (9)
Last ____ Home; Elrond's home (6)
Leader of the dwarves after Thorin (4)

Misty or Lonely (8)
Mr. Baggins (5)
Never leave the ___ in Mirkwood (4)
Never leave the path in this place (8)
Old watch post on SW side of mountain (9)
Pale-eyed water creature (6)
Raven; son of Carc (4)
Saved Thorin & Co. from the wargs & goblins (6)
Smaug's puff (5)
Smaug's sense of ___ was keen (5)
Tame messenger birds (8)
The Foe Hammer (9)
The ____ in Bilbo made him adventurous (4)
Thorin & Co. climbed in them to avoid wargs (5)
Town ruins in the shadow of the mountain (4)
Travelers left the path to see what was at these (6)
Travelers looked for the ___ entrance to the mountain (6)
Trolls turned to ___ in the sun (5)
Used to cross the black water (4)
Wizard (7)
___ & Beater; goblin names for Orcrist & Glamdring (5)
___ Mountain; where Smaug lived (6)
____ Lands; where Bilbo first wished he were home (4)
____ River; river in Mirkwood (5)
_____ Dragon Inn (5)
_____ Mountains (5)

The Hobbit Word Search 2 Answer Key

```
R  O     A  C  S  E  H  E     B        D              N        K           D
   T     D  M  T  S  A  S  I  A  E     C  I           I        G
B  O        M  A  P  G     G  L  A  M  D  R  I  N  G  N
   O        P  U  I  R  L  A  V  E  B     R  O        A  N  O  G
   K  A     G  A  N  E  E  R        B  O  A  H        M  I     R
S        T     W     S  S  N  R  O  I  F  B  T  E        T     L
B  T  R  A  V  E  N  H  I  L  L     T  S  I  K  E  Y  S     E
L  I  O        E  O  V  A        E  H  O  V        T  E  P
A  B        N  E  M  E     T  D  H  R  M  P     E     C  I
C  B        R  E  N     D  N  S  O  S     U  K        R  P
K  O  G  L  D  G  O        U  L     W  R  C  S  Y  Y  E  D
G  H  Y  E  O  O  A  R  O        B  U  O  T  L  T     T  U   T
O     L  Z  W     H  N  M     B  P  H  E  S        N  F  R
L  L  A  K     T  E     D  M     G  N  I     R  R  E  I
L  T  R  O  L  L        O  A  I  O  M     O  A  E     N
U  I  S  M  E  L  L  B     L  L        E  W  S
M  P  I  N  E  C  O  N  E  S     F  B  D  P  O  N  I  E  S
```

Battle of ____ Armies (4)
Bear-man (5)
Beorn loaned these as transportation for the travelers (6)
Bert or Tom, for example (5)
Bilbo took this item, which made Smaug angry (3)
Bilbo's name for his knife (5)
Bilbo's showed even when he wore the ring (6)
Bilbo's smoking device (4)
Bilbo, for example (6)
Biscuit-like food (4)
Dragon (5)
Dwalin, Bifur or Dori, for example (5)
Dwarves thought these creatures were foolish (5)
Elf New Year; ___'s Day (5)
Elrond was ___ of the Elves (4)
Evil wolves (5)
Gandalf gave Thorin this and a key (3)
Gandalf lit them on fire & threw them at wargs (9)
Goblin that killed Thorin's grandfather (4)
Gollum couldn't guess what was in Bilbo's ___ (7)
Gollum's birthday present that Bilbo found (4)
Got wet in the enchanted black water (6)
His grandfather was King of the Mountain (6)
It opened the secret door in the mountain (3)
Killed Smaug with a black arrow (4)
King of the Elves (6)
Lake town (8)
Land of the elves (9)
Last ____ Home; Elrond's home (6)
Leader of the dwarves after Thorin (4)

Misty or Lonely (8)
Mr. Baggins (5)
Never leave the ___ in Mirkwood (4)
Never leave the path in this place (8)
Old watch post on SW side of mountain (9)
Pale-eyed water creature (6)
Raven; son of Carc (4)
Saved Thorin & Co. from the wargs & goblins (6)
Smaug's puff (5)
Smaug's sense of ___ was keen (5)
Tame messenger birds (8)
The Foe Hammer (9)
The ____ in Bilbo made him adventurous (4)
Thorin & Co. climbed in them to avoid wargs (5)
Town ruins in the shadow of the mountain (4)
Travelers left the path to see what was at these (6)
Travelers looked for the ___ entrance to the mountain (6)
Trolls turned to ___ in the sun (5)
Used to cross the black water (4)
Wizard (7)
___ & Beater; goblin names for Orcrist & Glamdring (5)
___ Mountain; where Smaug lived (6)
____ Lands; where Bilbo first wished he were home (4)
____ River; river in Mirkwood (5)
_____ Dragon Inn (5)
_____ Mountains (5)

The Hobbit Word Search 3

```
P S L D K Y Y G P J T Y L P G M V T B L
O B S K C L S W K O R T D W A R F O O P
C X G L A E Z H S W N S B R N R X K A Q
K C J O L N A O A T C I C M D S H M T D
E U K S B O B G S D O M E D A S M O J T
T P T R O L L E L R O N D S L Q S U J N
S W R H I L I N I E I W E H F G P N G
E I E B O S B N C S N D R A U M I T G F
C L A T W R G F L G D R D D D D V
R S R O I T E L A B W L K V R I X
E I U E O X R N D B E L L E L R N G
T A E D V X T N S I O V P A S S E G
Y M E S E R K E M G R K D O Z S L M
K I G L P M W O H N I R U D O N D
S J T V D I K T T C Y R R I G L Y
T G E C E Y S P R E S L O J A K P R
I S V X S M X N G I W K D B S H L
N V I G R E N Z S M S L H O B B I C
G B F L B P L Y T O X N R P R O A J R
B O M B U R L P H P I N E C O N E S G S
```

AZOG	DURIN	KING	RAVENHILL	SWORDS
BARD	DWARF	LIGHTS	RIDDLES	THORIN
BARRELS	EAGLES	LONE	RING	TOLKIEN
BEORN	ELROND	LONELY	RIVENDELL	TOOK
BILBO	ELVES	MAP	ROAC	TREASURE
BITER	FIVE	MISTY	SECRET	TREES
BLACK	GANDALF	MOUNTAIN	SHADOW	TROLL
BOAT	GOBLIN	ORCRIST	SMAUG	WARGS
BOMBUR	GOLLUM	PATH	SMELL	WILLIAM
CRAM	GREEN	PINECONES	SMOKE	WOODELVES
CUP	HOBBIT	PIPE	SPIDERS	
DAIN	HOMELY	POCKETS	STING	
DALE	KEY	PONIES	STONE	

Copyrighted

The Hobbit Word Search 3 Answer Key

AZOG	DURIN	KING	RAVENHILL	SWORDS
BARD	DWARF	LIGHTS	RIDDLES	THORIN
BARRELS	EAGLES	LONE	RING	TOLKIEN
BEORN	ELROND	LONELY	RIVENDELL	TOOK
BILBO	ELVES	MAP	ROAC	TREASURE
BITER	FIVE	MISTY	SECRET	TREES
BLACK	GANDALF	MOUNTAIN	SHADOW	TROLL
BOAT	GOBLIN	ORCRIST	SMAUG	WARGS
BOMBUR	GOLLUM	PATH	SMELL	WILLIAM
CRAM	GREEN	PINECONES	SMOKE	WOODELVES
CUP	HOBBIT	PIPE	SPIDERS	
DAIN	HOMELY	POCKETS	STING	
DALE	KEY	PONIES	STONE	

The Hobbit Word Search 4

```
W O O D E L V E S N L S W O R D S H W M
T H R U S H E S T I L O M V M F E G A G
S W X N Y J Q H G E I V N N O C H E X R W
P O N I E S O H R D H A N E K P R T D G V
D D D A P R T R B W N R Z G L E Y T N S W
Q A L T I S A Q R A E K X O N Y I T D J
Q H V N N B S Z Q R V E H G T S L O Q H S
O S X U E Y M D V F A N H L L L O A R T
B L D O C T E H U R R S M P K G U A M M S
L Y O M O K L S D R X T P I V O X N W V
I W R N N Y L G A E I O E J N B Y E V G
B O A T E V I F L A D N A G B L A C K B
L O G K S Y M V E A R E G A E I P R V
C Q M R H H E T H O M D R M C N O O R D
K B X B E S Y L E S H D O M A R C M E S
O I K M U E M B R T T H R P O P K A F F
O T N T M R N I A O D O H I R Q E N S P
T E A G L E S P S C N A N P N D T C U J
B R H O B E B I T K T U D I E L G S E B
S P I D E R S M X R Y P F N S E C R E T
```

ARKENSTONE
AZOG
BARD
BARRELS
BEORN
BILBO
BITER
BLACK
BOAT
BOMBUR
CRAM
CUP
DAIN
DALE
DURIN
DWARF

EAGLES
ELROND
ELVES
FIVE
GANDALF
GLAMDRING
GOBLIN
GREEN
HOBBIT
HOMELY
KEY
KING
LIGHTS
LONE
LONELY
MAP

MISTY
MOUNTAIN
NECROMANCER
PATH
PINECONES
PIPE
POCKETS
PONIES
RAVENHILL
RING
ROAC
SECRET
SHADOW
SMAUG
SMELL
SMOKE

SPIDERS
STING
STONE
SWORDS
THORIN
THRUSHES
TOLKIEN
TOOK
TREASURE
TREES
TROLL
WARGS
WOODELVES

Copyrighted

The Hobbit Word Search 4 Answer Key

ARKENSTONE	EAGLES	MISTY	SPIDERS
AZOG	ELROND	MOUNTAIN	STING
BARD	ELVES	NECROMANCER	STONE
BARRELS	FIVE	PATH	SWORDS
BEORN	GANDALF	PINECONES	THORIN
BILBO	GLAMDRING	PIPE	THRUSHES
BITER	GOBLIN	POCKETS	TOLKIEN
BLACK	GREEN	PONIES	TOOK
BOAT	HOBBIT	RAVENHILL	TREASURE
BOMBUR	HOMELY	RING	TREES
CRAM	KEY	ROAC	TROLL
CUP	KING	SECRET	WARGS
DAIN	LIGHTS	SHADOW	WOODELVES
DALE	LONE	SMAUG	
DURIN	LONELY	SMELL	
DWARF	MAP	SMOKE	

The Hobbit Crossword 1

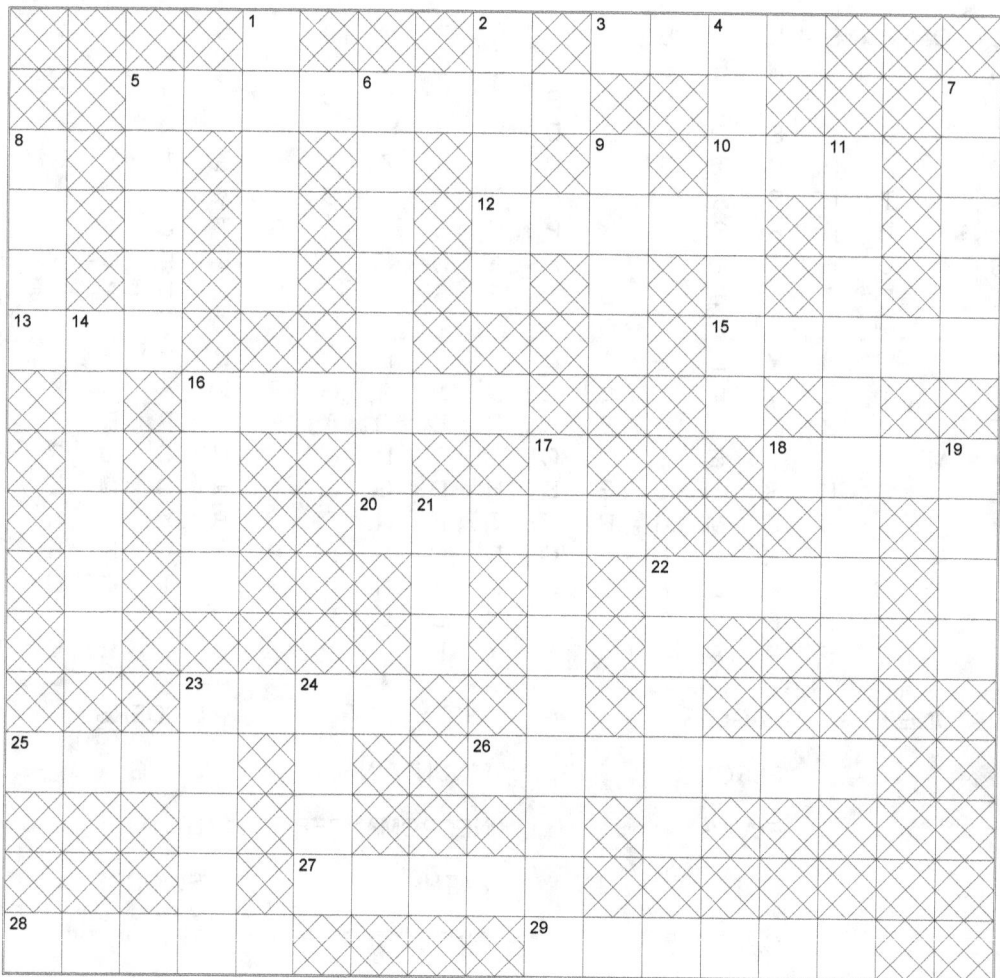

Across

3. Bilbo's smoking device
5. Misty or Lonely
10. Bilbo took this item, which made Smaug angry
12. ____ River; river in Mirkwood
13. It opened the secret door in the mountain
15. Thorin & Co. climbed in them to avoid wargs
16. Travelers left the path to see what was at these
18. Raven; son of Carc
20. Smaug's sense of ___ was keen
22. Town ruins in the shadow of the mountain
23. Used to cross the black water
25. Battle of ____ Armies
26. The Goblin Cleaver
27. _____ Dragon Inn
28. Trolls turned to ___ in the sun
29. Azog, for example

Down

1. Elf New Year; ___'s Day
2. Mr. Baggins
4. Gollum couldn't guess what was in Bilbo's ___
5. _____ Mountains
6. Tame messenger birds
7. Evil wolves
8. The ____ in Bilbo made him adventurous
9. Leader of the dwarves after Thorin
11. Gandalf lit them on fire & threw them at wargs
14. King of the Elves
16. ____ Lands; where Bilbo first wished he were home
17. The Foe Hammer
19. Biscuit-like food
21. Gandalf gave Thorin this and a key
22. Dwalin, Bifur or Dori, for example
23. Bear-man
24. Goblin that killed Thorin's grandfather

The Hobbit Crossword 1 Answer Key

			1 D		2 B		3 P	I	4 P	E		
		5 M	O	U	6 N	T	A	I	N			7 W
8 T		I		R	H		L		9 D		10 C	U	11 P	A
O		S		I	R		12 B	L	A	C	K		I	R
O		T		N	U		O		I		E		N	G
13 K	14 E	Y			S				N		15 T	R	E	E	S
	L		16 L	I	G	H	T	S			S		C	
	R		O				E		17 G			18 R	O	A	19 C
	O		N			20 S	M	21 E	L	L			N		R
	N		E				A		A		22 D	A	L	E	A
	D						P		M		W		S		M
			23 B	O	24 A	T			D		A			
25 F	I	V	E		Z			26 O	R	C	R	I	S	T
					O			I			F			
				27 G	R	E	E	N						
28 S	T	O	N	E				29 G	O	B	L	I	N	

Across

3. Bilbo's smoking device
5. Misty or Lonely
10. Bilbo took this item, which made Smaug angry
12. ____ River; river in Mirkwood
13. It opened the secret door in the mountain
15. Thorin & Co. climbed in them to avoid wargs
16. Travelers left the path to see what was at these
18. Raven; son of Carc
20. Smaug's sense of ___ was keen
22. Town ruins in the shadow of the mountain
23. Used to cross the black water
25. Battle of ____ Armies
26. The Goblin Cleaver
27. _____ Dragon Inn
28. Trolls turned to ___ in the sun
29. Azog, for example

Down

1. Elf New Year; ___'s Day
2. Mr. Baggins
4. Gollum couldn't guess what was in Bilbo's ___
5. _____ Mountains
6. Tame messenger birds
7. Evil wolves
8. The ____ in Bilbo made him adventurous
9. Leader of the dwarves after Thorin
11. Gandalf lit them on fire & threw them at wargs
14. King of the Elves
16. ____ Lands; where Bilbo first wished he were home
17. The Foe Hammer
19. Biscuit-like food
21. Gandalf gave Thorin this and a key
22. Dwalin, Bifur or Dori, for example
23. Bear-man
24. Goblin that killed Thorin's grandfather

The Hobbit Crossword 2

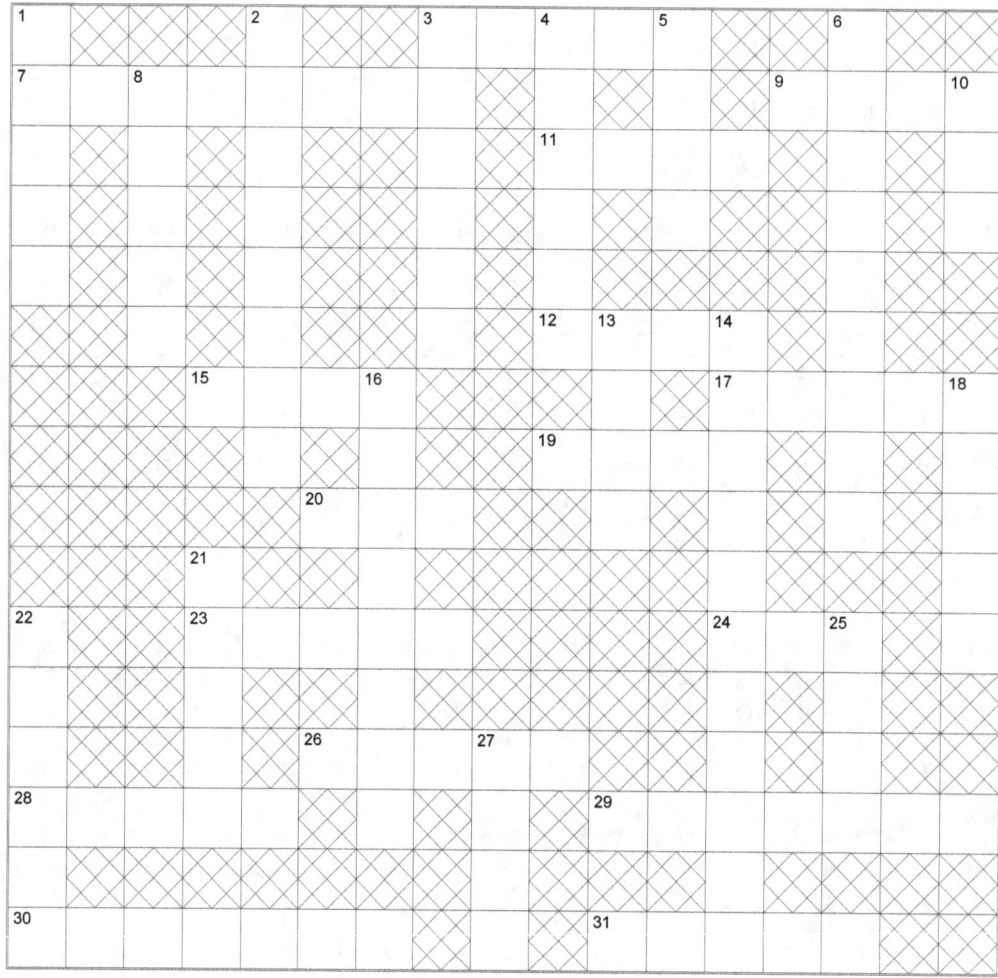

Across

3. Smaug's sense of ___ was keen
7. Lake town
9. The ____ in Bilbo made him adventurous
11. Gollum's birthday present that Bilbo found
12. Leader of the dwarves after Thorin
15. Biscuit-like food
17. Dwarves thought these creatures were foolish
19. Raven; son of Carc
20. Bilbo took this item, which made Smaug angry
23. _____ Mountains
24. Gandalf gave Thorin this and a key
26. Mr. Baggins
28. ___ & Beater; goblin names for Orcrist & Glamdring
29. Gollum couldn't guess what was in Bilbo's ___
30. Bilbo & Gollum's game
31. Evil wolves

Down

1. Bear-man
2. Smaug slept on it
3. Bilbo's showed even when he wore the ring
4. King of the Elves
5. ____ Lands; where Bilbo first wished he were home
6. Captured the dwarves & actually saved them
8. _____ Dragon Inn
10. It opened the secret door in the mountain
13. Goblin that killed Thorin's grandfather
14. Council of Wizards drove the ____ out of southern Mirkwood
16. Misty or Lonely
18. Trolls turned to ___ in the sun
21. Smaug's puff
22. Got wet in the enchanted black water
25. Bilbo's smoking device
27. Used to cross the black water

The Hobbit Crossword 2 Answer Key

	1 B		2 T		3 S	M	4 E	5 L		6 W	
7 E	S	8 G	A	R	O	T	H		L		9 T	O	O	10 K
	O		R		E			11 R	I	N	G		O		E
	R		E		A			O		E			D		Y
	N		E		S			O					E		
			N		U		W	12 D	13 A	I	14 N	L		
			15 C	R	A	16 M			Z		17 E	L	V	E	18 S
					E		O		19 R	O	A	C	E		T
					20 C	U	P		G		R	S			O
				21 S		N			O						N
22 B		23 M	I	S	T	Y				24 M	A	25 P		E
O		O		A						A		I		
M		K		26 B	I	L	27 B	O		N		P		
28 B	I	T	E	R		N		O		29 P	O	C	K	E	T	S
U								A		E			
30 R	I	D	D	L	E	S		T		31 W	A	R	G	S

Across
- 3. Smaug's sense of ___ was keen
- 7. Lake town
- 9. The ___ in Bilbo made him adventurous
- 11. Gollum's birthday present that Bilbo found
- 12. Leader of the dwarves after Thorin
- 15. Biscuit-like food
- 17. Dwarves thought these creatures were foolish
- 19. Raven; son of Carc
- 20. Bilbo took this item, which made Smaug angry
- 23. ___ Mountains
- 24. Gandalf gave Thorin this and a key
- 26. Mr. Baggins
- 28. ___ & Beater; goblin names for Orcrist & Glamdring
- 29. Gollum couldn't guess what was in Bilbo's ___
- 30. Bilbo & Gollum's game
- 31. Evil wolves

Down
- 1. Bear-man
- 2. Smaug slept on it
- 3. Bilbo's showed even when he wore the ring
- 4. King of the Elves
- 5. ___ Lands; where Bilbo first wished he were home
- 6. Captured the dwarves & actually saved them
- 8. ___ Dragon Inn
- 10. It opened the secret door in the mountain
- 13. Goblin that killed Thorin's grandfather
- 14. Council of Wizards drove the ___ out of southern Mirkwood
- 16. Misty or Lonely
- 18. Trolls turned to ___ in the sun
- 21. Smaug's puff
- 22. Got wet in the enchanted black water
- 25. Bilbo's smoking device
- 27. Used to cross the black water

The Hobbit Crossword 3

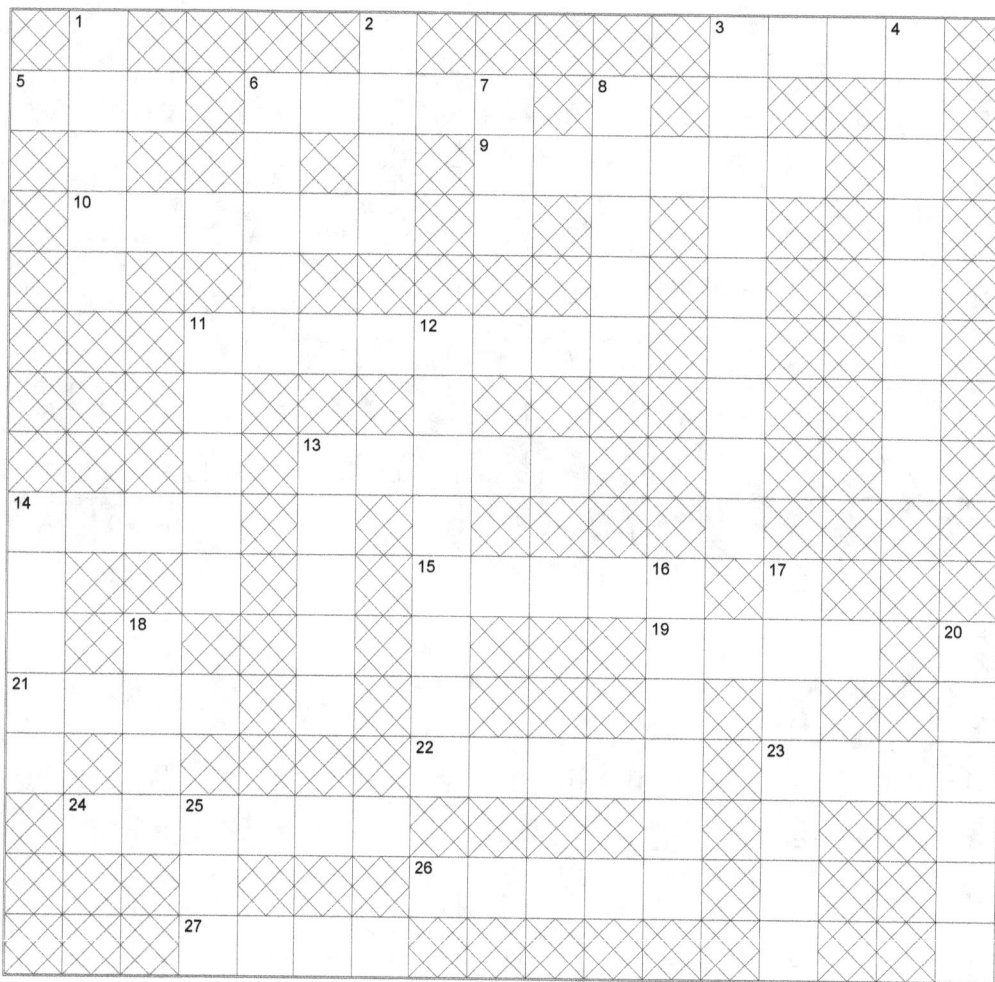

Across

3. Bilbo's smoking device
5. Gandalf gave Thorin this and a key
6. ____ River; river in Mirkwood
9. King of the Elves
10. Azog, for example
11. Misty or Lonely
13. Elf New Year; ___'s Day
14. Used to cross the black water
15. Trolls turned to ___ in the sun
19. Goblin that killed Thorin's grandfather
21. Raven; son of Carc
22. Smaug's sense of ___ was keen
23. Elrond was ___ of the Elves
24. Travelers looked for the ___ entrance to the mountain
26. Thorin & Co. climbed in them to avoid wargs
27. Never leave the ___ in Mirkwood

Down

1. Evil wolves
2. Leader of the dwarves after Thorin
3. Gandalf lit them on fire & threw them at wargs
4. Lake town
6. Mr. Baggins
7. It opened the secret door in the mountain
8. _____ Dragon Inn
11. _____ Mountains
12. Tame messenger birds
13. Dwalin, Bifur or Dori, for example
14. Bear-man
16. Saved Thorin & Co. from the wargs & goblins
17. Gollum couldn't guess what was in Bilbo's ___
18. Town ruins in the shadow of the mountain
20. Travelers left the path to see what was at these
25. Bilbo took this item, which made Smaug angry

The Hobbit Crossword 3 Answer Key

	1 W		2 D			3 P	I	P	4 E
5 M	A	P	6 B	L	A	C	K	8 G	I	S
	R		I			9 E	L	R	O	N	D	G
10 G	O	B	L	I	N		Y		E		A
	S		B				E		C		R
		11 M	O	U	N	12 T	A	I	N		O
		I			H				O		T
		S		13 D	U	R	I	N		E		H
14 B	O	A	T		W		U				S
E		Y			A		15 S	T	O	16 N	E		17 P
O		18 D			R		H				19 A	Z	O	G	20 L
21 R	O	A	C		F		E				G		C		I
N		L					22 S	M	E	L	L		23 K	I	N	G
		24 S	25 E	C	R	E	T				E		E		H
			U				26 T	R	E	E	S		T		T
			27 P	A	T	H							S		S

Across
3. Bilbo's smoking device
5. Gandalf gave Thorin this and a key
6. ____ River; river in Mirkwood
9. King of the Elves
10. Azog, for example
11. Misty or Lonely
13. Elf New Year; ___'s Day
14. Used to cross the black water
15. Trolls turned to ___ in the sun
19. Goblin that killed Thorin's grandfather
21. Raven; son of Carc
22. Smaug's sense of ___ was keen
23. Elrond was ___ of the Elves
24. Travelers looked for the ___ entrance to the mountain
26. Thorin & Co. climbed in them to avoid wargs
27. Never leave the ___ in Mirkwood

Down
1. Evil wolves
2. Leader of the dwarves after Thorin
3. Gandalf lit them on fire & threw them at wargs
4. Lake town
6. Mr. Baggins
7. It opened the secret door in the mountain
8. _____ Dragon Inn
11. _____ Mountains
12. Tame messenger birds
13. Dwalin, Bifur or Dori, for example
14. Bear-man
16. Saved Thorin & Co. from the wargs & goblins
17. Gollum couldn't guess what was in Bilbo's ___
18. Town ruins in the shadow of the mountain
20. Travelers left the path to see what was at these
25. Bilbo took this item, which made Smaug angry

The Hobbit Crossword 4

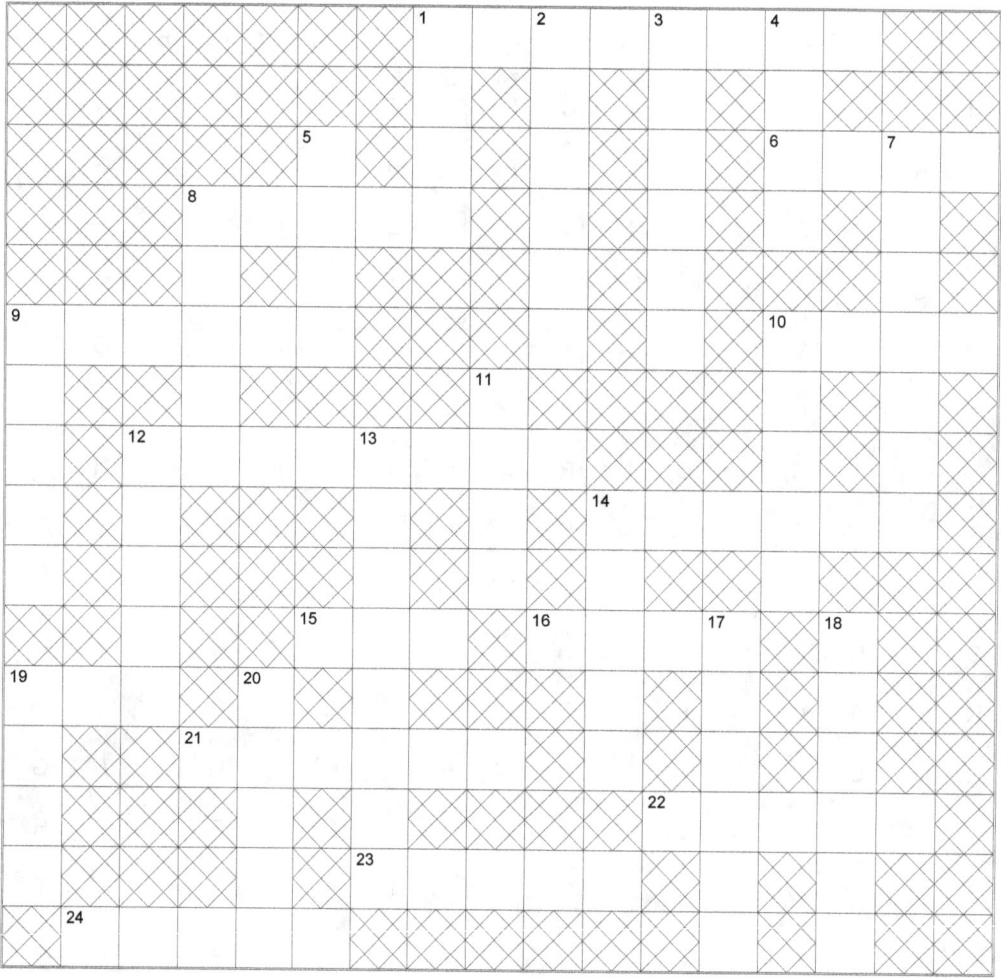

Across
1. Smaug slept on it
6. Goblin that killed Thorin's grandfather
8. ____ River; river in Mirkwood
9. Azog, for example
10. Killed Smaug with a black arrow
12. Misty or Lonely
14. Travelers looked for the ___ entrance to the mountain
15. Bilbo took this item, which made Smaug angry
16. ____ Lands; where Bilbo first wished he were home
19. It opened the secret door in the mountain
21. Travelers left the path to see what was at these
22. Dwarves thought these creatures were foolish
23. Smaug's sense of ___ was keen
24. Dwalin, Bifur or Dori, for example

Down
1. The ____ in Bilbo made him adventurous
2. King of the Elves
3. Bilbo's showed even when he wore the ring
4. Raven; son of Carc
5. Leader of the dwarves after Thorin
7. The Goblin Cleaver
8. Mr. Baggins
9. _____ Dragon Inn
10. Bear-man
11. Bilbo's smoking device
12. _____ Mountains
13. Tame messenger birds
14. Trolls turned to ___ in the sun
17. Saved Thorin & Co. from the wargs & goblins
18. Last ____ Home; Elrond's home
19. Elrond was ___ of the Elves
20. ___ & Beater; goblin names for Orcrist & Glamdring

The Hobbit Crossword 4 Answer Key

							1 T	2 R	E	A	3 S	U	4 R	E	
							O		L		H		O		
				5 D			O		R		A		6 A	Z	7 G
			8 B	L	A	C	K		O		D		C		R
			I		I				N		O				C
9 G	O	B	L	I	N				D		W		10 B	A	R	D
R			B				11 P						E		I
E		12 M	O	U	N	13 T	A	I	N				O		S
E		I				H		P		14 S	E	C	R	E	T
N		S				R		E		T			N		
		T			15 C	U	P		16 L	O	N	17 E		18 H	
19 K	E	Y		20 B		S			O			A		O	
I			21 L	I	G	H	T	S		E		G		M	
N				T			E					22 E	L	V	E	S
G				E		23 S	M	E	L	L		E		L	
	24 D	W	A	R	F							S		Y	

Across

1. Smaug slept on it
6. Goblin that killed Thorin's grandfather
8. ____ River; river in Mirkwood
9. Azog, for example
10. Killed Smaug with a black arrow
12. Misty or Lonely
14. Travelers looked for the ___ entrance to the mountain
15. Bilbo took this item, which made Smaug angry
16. ____ Lands; where Bilbo first wished he were home
19. It opened the secret door in the mountain
21. Travelers left the path to see what was at these
22. Dwarves thought these creatures were foolish
23. Smaug's sense of ___ was keen
24. Dwalin, Bifur or Dori, for example

Down

1. The ____ in Bilbo made him adventurous
2. King of the Elves
3. Bilbo's showed even when he wore the ring
4. Raven; son of Carc
5. Leader of the dwarves after Thorin
7. The Goblin Cleaver
8. Mr. Baggins
9. _____ Dragon Inn
10. Bear-man
11. Bilbo's smoking device
12. _____ Mountains
13. Tame messenger birds
14. Trolls turned to ___ in the sun
17. Saved Thorin & Co. from the wargs & goblins
18. Last ____ Home; Elrond's home
19. Elrond was ___ of the Elves
20. ___ & Beater; goblin names for Orcrist & Glamdring

The Hobbit

ARKENSTONE	GOLLUM	SMOKE	BITER	DAIN
TREASURE	MAP	FIVE	TREES	RAVENHILL
HOMELY	BILBO	FREE SPACE	POCKETS	BARRELS
ORCRIST	BOAT	PONIES	GOBLIN	EAGLES
SHADOW	BEORN	KING	RIVENDELL	GANDALF

The Hobbit

MOUNTAIN	WARGS	DALE	TOOK	PIPE
CRAM	SWORDS	BOMBUR	LIGHTS	LONE
BARD	SMAUG	FREE SPACE	CUP	STING
THORIN	PATH	SECRET	AZOG	NECROMANCER
MIRKWOOD	MISTY	BLACK	STONE	ELROND

The Hobbit

ELVES	LONE	BEORN	ESGAROTH	BARRELS
PIPE	SMOKE	HOMELY	ELROND	DALE
TREES	AZOG	FREE SPACE	BLACK	ARKENSTONE
STING	SMELL	BITER	EAGLES	BARD
TOOK	CUP	PATH	MIRKWOOD	POCKETS

The Hobbit

ROAC	BOAT	WARGS	DWARF	LONELY
HOBBIT	DAIN	NECKLACE	TOLKIEN	RAVENHILL
GOLLUM	SMAUG	FREE SPACE	SWORDS	FIVE
GLAMDRING	RING	KING	WILLIAM	MAP
MOUNTAIN	NECROMANCER	CRAM	STONE	LIGHTS

The Hobbit

RIVENDELL	LONELY	SMOKE	KEY	WARGS
HOMELY	CUP	ELROND	THORIN	PIPE
BEORN	HOBBIT	FREE SPACE	DAIN	ARKENSTONE
TROLL	TOLKIEN	MOUNTAIN	GOBLIN	SECRET
PATH	WOODELVES	BITER	TREES	MAP

The Hobbit

AZOG	BOMBUR	SMAUG	GREEN	BARRELS
TREASURE	THRUSHES	ESGAROTH	FIVE	GOLLUM
ORCRIST	MIRKWOOD	FREE SPACE	LONE	STING
GLAMDRING	RIDDLES	MISTY	ELVES	GANDALF
LIGHTS	SMELL	NECKLACE	BILBO	NECROMANCER

The Hobbit

SMELL	BITER	WARGS	SWORDS	KEY
THORIN	ARKENSTONE	SMOKE	RAVENHILL	STONE
MIRKWOOD	LIGHTS	FREE SPACE	ESGAROTH	SPIDERS
BARRELS	FIVE	RIVENDELL	CUP	GOLLUM
NECROMANCER	SMAUG	TREASURE	GOBLIN	MOUNTAIN

The Hobbit

ROAC	DAIN	HOBBIT	WOODELVES	RIDDLES
THRUSHES	MISTY	BOAT	ELROND	BARD
LONELY	BILBO	FREE SPACE	PATH	PIPE
PINECONES	EAGLES	TOOK	POCKETS	BEORN
DWARF	AZOG	CRAM	WILLIAM	SECRET

The Hobbit

PINECONES	LONELY	MISTY	BARRELS	TREES
PATH	BILBO	POCKETS	SWORDS	FIVE
MAP	NECROMANCER	FREE SPACE	SMAUG	TROLL
WOODELVES	TOLKIEN	GOLLUM	DURIN	AZOG
GOBLIN	ELROND	DALE	BITER	KEY

The Hobbit

LONE	DAIN	TOOK	RIVENDELL	MOUNTAIN
BOMBUR	MIRKWOOD	THRUSHES	SMOKE	STONE
SPIDERS	SECRET	FREE SPACE	SHADOW	NECKLACE
SMELL	DWARF	GLAMDRING	KING	STING
ROAC	GANDALF	THORIN	GREEN	RING

The Hobbit

SWORDS	THRUSHES	LIGHTS	CUP	BOMBUR
HOMELY	STONE	ELVES	TREASURE	WILLIAM
DAIN	WOODELVES	FREE SPACE	BILBO	RING
GLAMDRING	TROLL	PONIES	RIDDLES	PIPE
PINECONES	TOLKIEN	PATH	TREES	BEORN

The Hobbit

RIVENDELL	THORIN	BLACK	MISTY	SMOKE
NECROMANCER	STING	WARGS	POCKETS	HOBBIT
FIVE	MOUNTAIN	FREE SPACE	GANDALF	ROAC
LONELY	DURIN	MAP	SMAUG	LONE
TOOK	DALE	RAVENHILL	ARKENSTONE	SHADOW

The Hobbit

STING	ELVES	GREEN	NECKLACE	TROLL
MISTY	TREASURE	TOLKIEN	PIPE	KEY
GOLLUM	DAIN	FREE SPACE	ARKENSTONE	RING
MOUNTAIN	POCKETS	WILLIAM	GANDALF	NECROMANCER
SPIDERS	BITER	LIGHTS	BLACK	CUP

The Hobbit

TREES	ORCRIST	DALE	DURIN	BILBO
AZOG	GLAMDRING	FIVE	ELROND	BEORN
PATH	TOOK	FREE SPACE	BARRELS	SMAUG
DWARF	RIVENDELL	THRUSHES	MAP	WOODELVES
LONE	SMELL	THORIN	EAGLES	MIRKWOOD

The Hobbit

GREEN	DWARF	PINECONES	ESGAROTH	TROLL
TREES	STING	SPIDERS	SWORDS	BARRELS
ROAC	LONELY	FREE SPACE	BOAT	ARKENSTONE
SMOKE	MAP	GLAMDRING	MISTY	KING
LONE	MIRKWOOD	RAVENHILL	DALE	TREASURE

The Hobbit

DAIN	AZOG	BILBO	PATH	THRUSHES
BITER	ELVES	KEY	ORCRIST	WARGS
STONE	RIDDLES	FREE SPACE	SHADOW	NECKLACE
CUP	RING	WILLIAM	MOUNTAIN	BARD
EAGLES	TOOK	PONIES	HOBBIT	FIVE

The Hobbit

NECROMANCER	THORIN	ELVES	THRUSHES	SMOKE
GLAMDRING	MOUNTAIN	ARKENSTONE	DALE	LIGHTS
ROAC	TROLL	FREE SPACE	HOMELY	BARRELS
PATH	SWORDS	BOAT	KEY	ORCRIST
BITER	POCKETS	TOLKIEN	AZOG	LONE

The Hobbit

ESGAROTH	HOBBIT	TREASURE	RAVENHILL	DWARF
PIPE	LONELY	BILBO	STING	CRAM
KING	GREEN	FREE SPACE	BOMBUR	ELROND
MISTY	WOODELVES	NECKLACE	TOOK	STONE
WILLIAM	RIVENDELL	CUP	GANDALF	SECRET

The Hobbit

GANDALF	THRUSHES	WOODELVES	BLACK	BOMBUR
RING	PONIES	SHADOW	MAP	EAGLES
DWARF	AZOG	FREE SPACE	ROAC	GLAMDRING
ORCRIST	STONE	CUP	KEY	WARGS
LONE	CRAM	LONELY	ESGAROTH	WILLIAM

The Hobbit

BITER	ELVES	HOMELY	MISTY	GREEN
DALE	BILBO	GOLLUM	NECKLACE	TOOK
BOAT	TREASURE	FREE SPACE	MOUNTAIN	SMAUG
SMOKE	BARRELS	TREES	DAIN	GOBLIN
TOLKIEN	THORIN	SECRET	SPIDERS	LIGHTS

The Hobbit

KEY	SWORDS	HOMELY	LONELY	STONE
HOBBIT	BEORN	ELROND	SMAUG	TROLL
BOMBUR	BARRELS	FREE SPACE	AZOG	ROAC
DURIN	SHADOW	CUP	TOOK	ARKENSTONE
WOODELVES	GANDALF	MOUNTAIN	BLACK	PINECONES

The Hobbit

PONIES	NECKLACE	RIVENDELL	RING	GOBLIN
GLAMDRING	THORIN	ORCRIST	ELVES	CRAM
BILBO	THRUSHES	FREE SPACE	BARD	WILLIAM
TREASURE	TOLKIEN	RIDDLES	KING	NECROMANCER
LIGHTS	PATH	DAIN	LONE	TREES

The Hobbit

RIVENDELL	TREASURE	FIVE	ORCRIST	STING
MOUNTAIN	RAVENHILL	GOBLIN	ROAC	PATH
GOLLUM	HOMELY	FREE SPACE	BITER	KING
CRAM	SPIDERS	PINECONES	DWARF	NECROMANCER
WARGS	TREES	MIRKWOOD	GLAMDRING	DURIN

The Hobbit

ELVES	STONE	WILLIAM	SMELL	PONIES
MAP	BLACK	HOBBIT	DAIN	POCKETS
BARRELS	AZOG	FREE SPACE	BEORN	GANDALF
SMAUG	ARKENSTONE	RIDDLES	RING	TROLL
KEY	ESGAROTH	BOMBUR	WOODELVES	CUP

The Hobbit

LIGHTS	GREEN	CRAM	WARGS	SMELL
GLAMDRING	TROLL	GOBLIN	AZOG	RING
RIDDLES	LONELY	FREE SPACE	HOBBIT	SHADOW
KING	BLACK	ARKENSTONE	DAIN	ESGAROTH
POCKETS	EAGLES	TOOK	MISTY	WILLIAM

The Hobbit

TOLKIEN	GOLLUM	MAP	THRUSHES	FIVE
PONIES	BITER	MIRKWOOD	BOMBUR	ELVES
SECRET	BOAT	FREE SPACE	STING	LONE
KEY	HOMELY	GANDALF	DWARF	DURIN
SMAUG	BARD	SWORDS	PATH	PINECONES

The Hobbit

PIPE	SMAUG	BARD	RING	KEY
NECKLACE	TOLKIEN	GLAMDRING	RAVENHILL	CRAM
KING	SHADOW	FREE SPACE	MIRKWOOD	THORIN
GOBLIN	DURIN	LIGHTS	WILLIAM	SMOKE
LONELY	EAGLES	BOMBUR	RIVENDELL	TREES

The Hobbit

GREEN	ELROND	GANDALF	SPIDERS	STONE
POCKETS	THRUSHES	MAP	TOOK	SWORDS
FIVE	BEORN	FREE SPACE	ESGAROTH	ELVES
PATH	BILBO	LONE	BOAT	AZOG
HOBBIT	SMELL	WARGS	PINECONES	RIDDLES

The Hobbit

EAGLES	THRUSHES	KING	PINECONES	SHADOW
ELVES	BITER	THORIN	ROAC	BARD
BILBO	NECROMANCER	FREE SPACE	MISTY	ARKENSTONE
FIVE	TROLL	PIPE	BARRELS	WARGS
SECRET	WILLIAM	HOMELY	HOBBIT	RAVENHILL

The Hobbit

RIDDLES	ELROND	SWORDS	LONE	BOAT
DAIN	LIGHTS	POCKETS	TREASURE	MOUNTAIN
PONIES	SPIDERS	FREE SPACE	SMAUG	BOMBUR
CRAM	GANDALF	ORCRIST	STING	DURIN
TOLKIEN	CUP	STONE	MIRKWOOD	GOLLUM

The Hobbit

ELROND	LONELY	WILLIAM	SHADOW	BITER
NECKLACE	TOOK	DWARF	RIVENDELL	ELVES
THRUSHES	SMAUG	FREE SPACE	TREASURE	SMOKE
CUP	DAIN	BARD	MAP	BARRELS
BLACK	PONIES	GLAMDRING	KEY	GREEN

The Hobbit

ORCRIST	STONE	AZOG	GOLLUM	ESGAROTH
BOAT	EAGLES	RIDDLES	RING	MISTY
RAVENHILL	GANDALF	FREE SPACE	POCKETS	SWORDS
CRAM	HOBBIT	BOMBUR	GOBLIN	BILBO
PATH	SPIDERS	DALE	MOUNTAIN	LONE

The Hobbit Vocabulary Word List

No.	Word	Clue/Definition
1.	ABOMINABLE	Thoroughly unpleasant
2.	ABSURD	Ridiculous
3.	AMENDED	Corrected; made better
4.	ANTIQUITY	Quality of being very old or ancient
5.	ASTONISHED	Surprised
6.	AUDACIOUS	Daring; bold
7.	BUSTLE	Commotion; hurried activity
8.	CONSPIRATOR	One who joins in planning or plotting
9.	DELL	Small, secluded, wooded valley
10.	DEPREDATIONS	Acts of preying upon others
11.	DROUGHT	Long period of time with no rain
12.	DUBIOUS	Doubtful
13.	EDDYING	Going against the main current, especially in a swirling motion
14.	ENMITY	Deep hatred
15.	EXPEDITION	Journey undertaken with a definite objective
16.	EYRIE	Nest built on a high place
17.	GUARDIAN	One who guards, protects or defends
18.	HART	Male deer
19.	HINDER	Delay; get in the way of
20.	HOARD	A gathered, hidden, or stored supply or treasure
21.	HOIST	Lift up
22.	IMPENETRABLE	Can't be pierced or entered through
23.	IMPLORE	Ask or beg urgently
24.	INEVITABLE	Unavoidable
25.	INFURIATE	To make angry; enrage
26.	KIN	Relatives
27.	LARDERS	Pantry or cupboards containing food stores
28.	LOATHSOME	Repulsive; disgusting
29.	LURE	Entice; attract
30.	MARAUDING	Wandering in search of something to steal
31.	MEMOIRS	Narrative of experiences an author has lived through
32.	MUSTERING	Gathering
33.	PERILOUS	Dangerous
34.	PERISH	Die; pass from existence
35.	PERPETUALLY	Continuously; always
36.	PINNACLE	Top; high point
37.	PLIGHT	Situation of difficulty
38.	PLUNDER	Stolen property
39.	PRECISE	Exact
40.	PREFER	To like better; rather
41.	PURSUING	Chasing
42.	QUAY	Wharf of reinforced bank where ships are loaded
43.	QUEST	Search
44.	RANSOM	Release, give up or free in return for payment
45.	REMUNERATION	Payment
46.	REPOSE	Rest
47.	REQUISITE	Required, necessary
48.	RUNES	Words written in ancient Germanic letters
49.	SEIZED	Grabbed
50.	SORCEROUS	In command of magic, spells and witchcraft
51.	SUSPICION	Thinking something exists, especially something wrong, without

	any proof
52. TUNIC	Long, loose-fitting shirt or coat
53. UNCANNY	Unexplainable and strange, exciting wonder and fear
54. UNIMPEACHABLE	Beyond all doubt; unquestionable
55. VAIN	Lacking substance; hollow; fruitless
56. WANING	Lessening; going away; ending
57. WILY	Calculating; plotting
58. WROUGHT	Shaped; worked

The Hobbit Vocabulary Fill In The Blanks 1

_____ 1. To make angry; enrage

_____ 2. Required, necessary

_____ 3. Wharf of reinforced bank where ships are loaded

_____ 4. Thoroughly unpleasant

_____ 5. Top; high point

_____ 6. Lessening; going away; ending

_____ 7. Ask or beg urgently

_____ 8. Surprised

_____ 9. Grabbed

_____ 10. Relatives

_____ 11. Wandering in search of something to steal

_____ 12. Shaped; worked

_____ 13. Small, secluded, wooded valley

_____ 14. Rest

_____ 15. Pantry or cupboards containing food stores

_____ 16. Words written in ancient Germanic letters

_____ 17. To like better; rather

_____ 18. Situation of difficulty

_____ 19. Ridiculous

_____ 20. Repulsive; disgusting

The Hobbit Vocabulary Fill In The Blanks 1 Answer Key

INFURIATE	1. To make angry; enrage
REQUISITE	2. Required, necessary
QUAY	3. Wharf of reinforced bank where ships are loaded
ABOMINABLE	4. Thoroughly unpleasant
PINNACLE	5. Top; high point
WANING	6. Lessening; going away; ending
IMPLORE	7. Ask or beg urgently
ASTONISHED	8. Surprised
SEIZED	9. Grabbed
KIN	10. Relatives
MARAUDING	11. Wandering in search of something to steal
WROUGHT	12. Shaped; worked
DELL	13. Small, secluded, wooded valley
REPOSE	14. Rest
LARDERS	15. Pantry or cupboards containing food stores
RUNES	16. Words written in ancient Germanic letters
PREFER	17. To like better; rather
PLIGHT	18. Situation of difficulty
ABSURD	19. Ridiculous
LOATHSOME	20. Repulsive; disgusting

The Hobbit Vocabulary Fill In The Blanks 2

_____ 1. Going against the main current, especially in a swirling motion

_____ 2. Entice; attract

_____ 3. Gathering

_____ 4. Delay; get in the way of

_____ 5. Wandering in search of something to steal

_____ 6. Doubtful

_____ 7. Journey undertaken with a definite objective

_____ 8. Daring; bold

_____ 9. One who joins in planning or plotting

_____ 10. Situation of difficulty

_____ 11. Long period of time with no rain

_____ 12. Required, necessary

_____ 13. To like better; rather

_____ 14. One who guards, protects or defends

_____ 15. Long, loose-fitting shirt or coat

_____ 16. Rest

_____ 17. Surprised

_____ 18. Lacking substance; hollow; fruitless

_____ 19. Deep hatred

_____ 20. Narrative of experiences an author has lived through

The Hobbit Vocabulary Fill In The Blanks 2 Answer Key

EDDYING	1. Going against the main current, especially in a swirling motion
LURE	2. Entice; attract
MUSTERING	3. Gathering
HINDER	4. Delay; get in the way of
MARAUDING	5. Wandering in search of something to steal
DUBIOUS	6. Doubtful
EXPEDITION	7. Journey undertaken with a definite objective
AUDACIOUS	8. Daring; bold
CONSPIRATOR	9. One who joins in planning or plotting
PLIGHT	10. Situation of difficulty
DROUGHT	11. Long period of time with no rain
REQUISITE	12. Required, necessary
PREFER	13. To like better; rather
GUARDIAN	14. One who guards, protects or defends
TUNIC	15. Long, loose-fitting shirt or coat
REPOSE	16. Rest
ASTONISHED	17. Surprised
VAIN	18. Lacking substance; hollow; fruitless
ENMITY	19. Deep hatred
MEMOIRS	20. Narrative of experiences an author has lived through

The Hobbit Vocabulary Fill In The Blanks 3

_____ 1. Can't be pierced or entered through

_____ 2. Delay; get in the way of

_____ 3. Chasing

_____ 4. Nest built on a high place

_____ 5. Lacking substance; hollow; fruitless

_____ 6. Thinking something exists, especially something wrong, without any proof

_____ 7. Grabbed

_____ 8. Payment

_____ 9. Beyond all doubt; unquestionable

_____ 10. Stolen property

_____ 11. Pantry or cupboards containing food stores

_____ 12. A gathered, hidden, or stored supply or treasure

_____ 13. Small, secluded, wooded valley

_____ 14. Relatives

_____ 15. Wharf of reinforced bank where ships are loaded

_____ 16. Quality of being very old or ancient

_____ 17. Unavoidable

_____ 18. Situation of difficulty

_____ 19. Going against the main current, especially in a swirling motion

_____ 20. Lift up

The Hobbit Vocabulary Fill In The Blanks 3 Answer Key

IMPENETRABLE	1. Can't be pierced or entered through
HINDER	2. Delay; get in the way of
PURSUING	3. Chasing
EYRIE	4. Nest built on a high place
VAIN	5. Lacking substance; hollow; fruitless
SUSPICION	6. Thinking something exists, especially something wrong, without any proof
SEIZED	7. Grabbed
REMUNERATION	8. Payment
UNIMPEACHABLE	9. Beyond all doubt; unquestionable
PLUNDER	10. Stolen property
LARDERS	11. Pantry or cupboards containing food stores
HOARD	12. A gathered, hidden, or stored supply or treasure
DELL	13. Small, secluded, wooded valley
KIN	14. Relatives
QUAY	15. Wharf of reinforced bank where ships are loaded
ANTIQUITY	16. Quality of being very old or ancient
INEVITABLE	17. Unavoidable
PLIGHT	18. Situation of difficulty
EDDYING	19. Going against the main current, especially in a swirling motion
HOIST	20. Lift up

The Hobbit Vocabulary Fill In The Blanks 4

_____ 1. Rest

_____ 2. Dangerous

_____ 3. Payment

_____ 4. Lessening; going away; ending

_____ 5. Pantry or cupboards containing food stores

_____ 6. Grabbed

_____ 7. Can't be pierced or entered through

_____ 8. Daring; bold

_____ 9. Repulsive; disgusting

_____ 10. Chasing

_____ 11. A gathered, hidden, or stored supply or treasure

_____ 12. To like better; rather

_____ 13. Unexplainable and strange, exciting wonder and fear

_____ 14. Relatives

_____ 15. Quality of being very old or ancient

_____ 16. Wharf of reinforced bank where ships are loaded

_____ 17. Beyond all doubt; unquestionable

_____ 18. Ridiculous

_____ 19. Ask or beg urgently

_____ 20. Shaped; worked

The Hobbit Vocabulary Fill In The Blanks 4 Answer Key

REPOSE	1. Rest
PERILOUS	2. Dangerous
REMUNERATION	3. Payment
WANING	4. Lessening; going away; ending
LARDERS	5. Pantry or cupboards containing food stores
SEIZED	6. Grabbed
IMPENETRABLE	7. Can't be pierced or entered through
AUDACIOUS	8. Daring; bold
LOATHSOME	9. Repulsive; disgusting
PURSUING	10. Chasing
HOARD	11. A gathered, hidden, or stored supply or treasure
PREFER	12. To like better; rather
UNCANNY	13. Unexplainable and strange, exciting wonder and fear
KIN	14. Relatives
ANTIQUITY	15. Quality of being very old or ancient
QUAY	16. Wharf of reinforced bank where ships are loaded
UNIMPEACHABLE	17. Beyond all doubt; unquestionable
ABSURD	18. Ridiculous
IMPLORE	19. Ask or beg urgently
WROUGHT	20. Shaped; worked

The Hobbit Vocabulary Matching 1

___ 1. CONSPIRATOR   A. Thoroughly unpleasant
___ 2. ANTIQUITY   B. One who joins in planning or plotting
___ 3. KIN   C. Pantry or cupboards containing food stores
___ 4. PINNACLE   D. Chasing
___ 5. EYRIE   E. Commotion; hurried activity
___ 6. MUSTERING   F. Small, secluded, wooded valley
___ 7. ABOMINABLE   G. A gathered, hidden, or stored supply or treasure
___ 8. INFURIATE   H. Acts of preying upon others
___ 9. PRECISE   I. Daring; bold
___10. LARDERS   J. Search
___11. GUARDIAN   K. Continuously; always
___12. BUSTLE   L. Quality of being very old or ancient
___13. QUAY   M. Entice; attract
___14. LURE   N. Wharf of reinforced bank where ships are loaded
___15. PERILOUS   O. Situation of difficulty
___16. QUEST   P. Exact
___17. HOARD   Q. Required, necessary
___18. DELL   R. Nest built on a high place
___19. REQUISITE   S. Relatives
___20. PLIGHT   T. Narrative of experiences an author has lived through
___21. MEMOIRS   U. To make angry; enrage
___22. AUDACIOUS   V. Top; high point
___23. PURSUING   W. Gathering
___24. DEPREDATIONS   X. Dangerous
___25. PERPETUALLY   Y. One who guards, protects or defends

The Hobbit Vocabulary Matching 1 Answer Key

B - 1.	CONSPIRATOR	A. Thoroughly unpleasant
L - 2.	ANTIQUITY	B. One who joins in planning or plotting
S - 3.	KIN	C. Pantry or cupboards containing food stores
V - 4.	PINNACLE	D. Chasing
R - 5.	EYRIE	E. Commotion; hurried activity
W - 6.	MUSTERING	F. Small, secluded, wooded valley
A - 7.	ABOMINABLE	G. A gathered, hidden, or stored supply or treasure
U - 8.	INFURIATE	H. Acts of preying upon others
P - 9.	PRECISE	I. Daring; bold
C - 10.	LARDERS	J. Search
Y - 11.	GUARDIAN	K. Continuously; always
E - 12.	BUSTLE	L. Quality of being very old or ancient
N - 13.	QUAY	M. Entice; attract
M - 14.	LURE	N. Wharf of reinforced bank where ships are loaded
X - 15.	PERILOUS	O. Situation of difficulty
J - 16.	QUEST	P. Exact
G - 17.	HOARD	Q. Required, necessary
F - 18.	DELL	R. Nest built on a high place
Q - 19.	REQUISITE	S. Relatives
O - 20.	PLIGHT	T. Narrative of experiences an author has lived through
T - 21.	MEMOIRS	U. To make angry; enrage
I - 22.	AUDACIOUS	V. Top; high point
D - 23.	PURSUING	W. Gathering
H - 24.	DEPREDATIONS	X. Dangerous
K - 25.	PERPETUALLY	Y. One who guards, protects or defends

The Hobbit Vocabulary Matching 2

___ 1. ANTIQUITY   A. Continuously; always
___ 2. EDDYING   B. Deep hatred
___ 3. WROUGHT   C. Payment
___ 4. WANING   D. Going against the main current, especially in a swirling motion
___ 5. HOARD   E. Lacking substance; hollow; fruitless
___ 6. INEVITABLE   F. Journey undertaken with a definite objective
___ 7. REQUISITE   G. Entice; attract
___ 8. IMPENETRABLE   H. Surprised
___ 9. TUNIC   I. Lessening; going away; ending
___ 10. REMUNERATION   J. Gathering
___ 11. MUSTERING   K. Calculating; plotting
___ 12. PURSUING   L. A gathered, hidden, or stored supply or treasure
___ 13. ENMITY   M. Exact
___ 14. PRECISE   N. Required, necessary
___ 15. PERILOUS   O. Unavoidable
___ 16. WILY   P. Release, give up or free in return for payment
___ 17. HART   Q. Quality of being very old or ancient
___ 18. LURE   R. Repulsive; disgusting
___ 19. PERPETUALLY   S. Male deer
___ 20. RANSOM   T. Long, loose-fitting shirt or coat
___ 21. ASTONISHED   U. Corrected; made better
___ 22. VAIN   V. Chasing
___ 23. LOATHSOME   W. Dangerous
___ 24. AMENDED   X. Shaped; worked
___ 25. EXPEDITION   Y. Can't be pierced or entered through

The Hobbit Vocabulary Matching 2 Answer Key

Q - 1. ANTIQUITY		A. Continuously; always
D - 2. EDDYING		B. Deep hatred
X - 3. WROUGHT		C. Payment
I - 4. WANING		D. Going against the main current, especially in a swirling motion
L - 5. HOARD		E. Lacking substance; hollow; fruitless
O - 6. INEVITABLE		F. Journey undertaken with a definite objective
N - 7. REQUISITE		G. Entice; attract
Y - 8. IMPENETRABLE		H. Surprised
T - 9. TUNIC		I. Lessening; going away; ending
C - 10. REMUNERATION		J. Gathering
J - 11. MUSTERING		K. Calculating; plotting
V - 12. PURSUING		L. A gathered, hidden, or stored supply or treasure
B - 13. ENMITY		M. Exact
M - 14. PRECISE		N. Required, necessary
W - 15. PERILOUS		O. Unavoidable
K - 16. WILY		P. Release, give up or free in return for payment
S - 17. HART		Q. Quality of being very old or ancient
G - 18. LURE		R. Repulsive; disgusting
A - 19. PERPETUALLY		S. Male deer
P - 20. RANSOM		T. Long, loose-fitting shirt or coat
H - 21. ASTONISHED		U. Corrected; made better
E - 22. VAIN		V. Chasing
R - 23. LOATHSOME		W. Dangerous
U - 24. AMENDED		X. Shaped; worked
F - 25. EXPEDITION		Y. Can't be pierced or entered through

The Hobbit Vocabulary Matching 3

___ 1. DEPREDATIONS   A. In command of magic, spells and witchcraft
___ 2. MUSTERING   B. Journey undertaken with a definite objective
___ 3. PERILOUS   C. Male deer
___ 4. DUBIOUS   D. To like better; rather
___ 5. SUSPICION   E. Wandering in search of something to steal
___ 6. ABOMINABLE   F. Acts of preying upon others
___ 7. TUNIC   G. Die; pass from existence
___ 8. REQUISITE   H. Dangerous
___ 9. EXPEDITION   I. Relatives
___10. PREFER   J. Thinking something exists, especially something wrong, without any proof
___11. WANING   K. Repulsive; disgusting
___12. WILY   L. Doubtful
___13. HART   M. Calculating; plotting
___14. AUDACIOUS   N. Thoroughly unpleasant
___15. ASTONISHED   O. Long, loose-fitting shirt or coat
___16. PERPETUALLY   P. Beyond all doubt; unquestionable
___17. INEVITABLE   Q. Lessening; going away; ending
___18. RUNES   R. Words written in ancient Germanic letters
___19. SORCEROUS   S. Daring; bold
___20. LOATHSOME   T. Continuously; always
___21. KIN   U. Required, necessary
___22. UNIMPEACHABLE   V. Gathering
___23. MARAUDING   W. Top; high point
___24. PERISH   X. Surprised
___25. PINNACLE   Y. Unavoidable

The Hobbit Vocabulary Matching 3 Answer Key

F - 1. DEPREDATIONS
V - 2. MUSTERING
H - 3. PERILOUS
L - 4. DUBIOUS
J - 5. SUSPICION
N - 6. ABOMINABLE
O - 7. TUNIC
U - 8. REQUISITE
B - 9. EXPEDITION
D - 10. PREFER
Q - 11. WANING
M - 12. WILY
C - 13. HART
S - 14. AUDACIOUS
X - 15. ASTONISHED
T - 16. PERPETUALLY
Y - 17. INEVITABLE
R - 18. RUNES
A - 19. SORCEROUS
K - 20. LOATHSOME
I - 21. KIN
P - 22. UNIMPEACHABLE
E - 23. MARAUDING
G - 24. PERISH
W - 25. PINNACLE

A. In command of magic, spells and witchcraft
B. Journey undertaken with a definite objective
C. Male deer
D. To like better; rather
E. Wandering in search of something to steal
F. Acts of preying upon others
G. Die; pass from existence
H. Dangerous
I. Relatives
J. Thinking something exists, especially something wrong, without any proof
K. Repulsive; disgusting
L. Doubtful
M. Calculating; plotting
N. Thoroughly unpleasant
O. Long, loose-fitting shirt or coat
P. Beyond all doubt; unquestionable
Q. Lessening; going away; ending
R. Words written in ancient Germanic letters
S. Daring; bold
T. Continuously; always
U. Required, necessary
V. Gathering
W. Top; high point
X. Surprised
Y. Unavoidable

The Hobbit Vocabulary Matching 4

___ 1. HINDER   A. Dangerous
___ 2. REQUISITE   B. Die; pass from existence
___ 3. LOATHSOME   C. Long, loose-fitting shirt or coat
___ 4. PERPETUALLY   D. Quality of being very old or ancient
___ 5. RUNES   E. Delay; get in the way of
___ 6. PRECISE   F. Lacking substance; hollow; fruitless
___ 7. VAIN   G. Ask or beg urgently
___ 8. ASTONISHED   H. Surprised
___ 9. PINNACLE   I. Top; high point
___10. EYRIE   J. Words written in ancient Germanic letters
___11. TUNIC   K. Beyond all doubt; unquestionable
___12. RANSOM   L. Exact
___13. PERILOUS   M. Entice; attract
___14. PLUNDER   N. Thoroughly unpleasant
___15. ABOMINABLE   O. Continuously; always
___16. ANTIQUITY   P. A gathered, hidden, or stored supply or treasure
___17. UNIMPEACHABLE Q. Release, give up or free in return for payment
___18. WROUGHT   R. Stolen property
___19. QUAY   S. Wharf of reinforced bank where ships are loaded
___20. IMPLORE   T. Deep hatred
___21. EXPEDITION   U. Nest built on a high place
___22. PERISH   V. Shaped; worked
___23. HOARD   W. Required, necessary
___24. ENMITY   X. Journey undertaken with a definite objective
___25. LURE   Y. Repulsive; disgusting

The Hobbit Vocabulary Matching 4 Answer Key

E - 1. HINDER	A. Dangerous
W - 2. REQUISITE	B. Die; pass from existence
Y - 3. LOATHSOME	C. Long, loose-fitting shirt or coat
O - 4. PERPETUALLY	D. Quality of being very old or ancient
J - 5. RUNES	E. Delay; get in the way of
L - 6. PRECISE	F. Lacking substance; hollow; fruitless
F - 7. VAIN	G. Ask or beg urgently
H - 8. ASTONISHED	H. Surprised
I - 9. PINNACLE	I. Top; high point
U - 10. EYRIE	J. Words written in ancient Germanic letters
C - 11. TUNIC	K. Beyond all doubt; unquestionable
Q - 12. RANSOM	L. Exact
A - 13. PERILOUS	M. Entice; attract
R - 14. PLUNDER	N. Thoroughly unpleasant
N - 15. ABOMINABLE	O. Continuously; always
D - 16. ANTIQUITY	P. A gathered, hidden, or stored supply or treasure
K - 17. UNIMPEACHABLE	Q. Release, give up or free in return for payment
V - 18. WROUGHT	R. Stolen property
S - 19. QUAY	S. Wharf of reinforced bank where ships are loaded
G - 20. IMPLORE	T. Deep hatred
X - 21. EXPEDITION	U. Nest built on a high place
B - 22. PERISH	V. Shaped; worked
P - 23. HOARD	W. Required, necessary
T - 24. ENMITY	X. Journey undertaken with a definite objective
M - 25. LURE	Y. Repulsive; disgusting

The Hobbit Vocabulary Magic Squares 1

Match the definition with the vocabulary word. Put your answers in the magic squares below. When your answers are correct, all columns and rows will add to the same number.

A. EDDYING
B. HOIST
C. INEVITABLE
D. REPOSE
E. WILY
F. INFURIATE
G. MEMOIRS
H. BUSTLE
I. ASTONISHED
J. IMPENETRABLE
K. PLUNDER
L. DELL
M. QUEST
N. PINNACLE
O. HINDER
P. ABSURD

1. Lift up
2. Narrative of experiences an author has lived through
3. Stolen property
4. Top; high point
5. Search
6. Small, secluded, wooded valley
7. Commotion; hurried activity
8. Going against the main current, especially in a swirling motion
9. Ridiculous
10. Surprised
11. Calculating; plotting
12. Rest
13. Unavoidable
14. To make angry; enrage
15. Can't be pierced or entered through
16. Delay; get in the way of

A=	B=	C=	D=
E=	F=	G=	H=
I=	J=	K=	L=
M=	N=	O=	P=

The Hobbit Vocabulary Magic Squares 1 Answer Key

Match the definition with the vocabulary word. Put your answers in the magic squares below. When your answers are correct, all columns and rows will add to the same number.

A. EDDYING
B. HOIST
C. INEVITABLE
D. REPOSE
E. WILY
F. INFURIATE
G. MEMOIRS
H. BUSTLE
I. ASTONISHED
J. IMPENETRABLE
K. PLUNDER
L. DELL
M. QUEST
N. PINNACLE
O. HINDER
P. ABSURD

1. Lift up
2. Narrative of experiences an author has lived through
3. Stolen property
4. Top; high point
5. Search
6. Small, secluded, wooded valley
7. Commotion; hurried activity
8. Going against the main current, especially in a swirling motion
9. Ridiculous
10. Surprised
11. Calculating; plotting
12. Rest
13. Unavoidable
14. To make angry; enrage
15. Can't be pierced or entered through
16. Delay; get in the way of

A=8	B=1	C=13	D=12
E=11	F=14	G=2	H=7
I=10	J=15	K=3	L=6
M=5	N=4	O=16	P=9

The Hobbit Vocabulary Magic Squares 2

Match the definition with the vocabulary word. Put your answers in the magic squares below. When your answers are correct, all columns and rows will add to the same number.

A. AMENDED
B. PREFER
C. SEIZED
D. LOATHSOME
E. WROUGHT
F. EXPEDITION
G. PERILOUS
H. TUNIC
I. BUSTLE
J. ABSURD
K. EYRIE
L. QUEST
M. HART
N. SUSPICION
O. PERPETUALLY
P. GUARDIAN

1. Long, loose-fitting shirt or coat
2. Corrected; made better
3. To like better; rather
4. Dangerous
5. Ridiculous
6. Continuously; always
7. One who guards, protects or defends
8. Commotion; hurried activity
9. Nest built on a high place
10. Thinking something exists, especially something wrong, without any proof
11. Male deer
12. Search
13. Shaped; worked
14. Repulsive; disgusting
15. Grabbed
16. Journey undertaken with a definite objective

A=	B=	C=	D=
E=	F=	G=	H=
I=	J=	K=	L=
M=	N=	O=	P=

The Hobbit Vocabulary Magic Squares 2 Answer Key

Match the definition with the vocabulary word. Put your answers in the magic squares below. When your answers are correct, all columns and rows will add to the same number.

A. AMENDED
B. PREFER
C. SEIZED
D. LOATHSOME
E. WROUGHT
F. EXPEDITION
G. PERILOUS
H. TUNIC
I. BUSTLE
J. ABSURD
K. EYRIE
L. QUEST
M. HART
N. SUSPICION
O. PERPETUALLY
P. GUARDIAN

1. Long, loose-fitting shirt or coat
2. Corrected; made better
3. To like better; rather
4. Dangerous
5. Ridiculous
6. Continuously; always
7. One who guards, protects or defends
8. Commotion; hurried activity
9. Nest built on a high place
10. Thinking something exists, especially something wrong, without any proof
11. Male deer
12. Search
13. Shaped; worked
14. Repulsive; disgusting
15. Grabbed
16. Journey undertaken with a definite objective

A=2	B=3	C=15	D=14
E=13	F=16	G=4	H=1
I=8	J=5	K=9	L=12
M=11	N=10	O=6	P=7

The Hobbit Vocabulary Magic Squares 3

Match the definition with the vocabulary word. Put your answers in the magic squares below. When your answers are correct, all columns and rows will add to the same number.

A. VAIN
B. WANING
C. EDDYING
D. PURSUING
E. ANTIQUITY
F. LARDERS
G. PLUNDER
H. PERPETUALLY
I. PERISH
J. ABSURD
K. LOATHSOME
L. PREFER
M. WILY
N. SORCEROUS
O. REQUISITE
P. EYRIE

1. Pantry or cupboards containing food stores
2. Die; pass from existence
3. Required, necessary
4. Chasing
5. Calculating; plotting
6. Lessening; going away; ending
7. Continuously; always
8. Repulsive; disgusting
9. Going against the main current, especially in a swirling motion
10. Nest built on a high place
11. Ridiculous
12. Quality of being very old or ancient
13. To like better; rather
14. Stolen property
15. Lacking substance; hollow; fruitless
16. In command of magic, spells and witchcraft

A=	B=	C=	D=
E=	F=	G=	H=
I=	J=	K=	L=
M=	N=	O=	P=

The Hobbit Vocabulary Magic Squares 3 Answer Key

Match the definition with the vocabulary word. Put your answers in the magic squares below. When your answers are correct, all columns and rows will add to the same number.

A. VAIN
B. WANING
C. EDDYING
D. PURSUING
E. ANTIQUITY
F. LARDERS
G. PLUNDER
H. PERPETUALLY
I. PERISH
J. ABSURD
K. LOATHSOME
L. PREFER
M. WILY
N. SORCEROUS
O. REQUISITE
P. EYRIE

1. Pantry or cupboards containing food stores
2. Die; pass from existence
3. Required, necessary
4. Chasing
5. Calculating; plotting
6. Lessening; going away; ending
7. Continuously; always
8. Repulsive; disgusting
9. Going against the main current, especially in a swirling motion
10. Nest built on a high place
11. Ridiculous
12. Quality of being very old or ancient
13. To like better; rather
14. Stolen property
15. Lacking substance; hollow; fruitless
16. In command of magic, spells and witchcraft

A=15	B=6	C=9	D=4
E=12	F=1	G=14	H=7
I=2	J=11	K=8	L=13
M=5	N=16	O=3	P=10

The Hobbit Vocabulary Magic Squares 4

Match the definition with the vocabulary word. Put your answers in the magic squares below. When your answers are correct, all columns and rows will add to the same number.

A. EXPEDITION
B. RUNES
C. GUARDIAN
D. PINNACLE
E. SORCEROUS
F. WILY
G. ABSURD
H. SUSPICION
I. ENMITY
J. KIN
K. TUNIC
L. AMENDED
M. REMUNERATION
N. INEVITABLE
O. HINDER
P. WANING

1. One who guards, protects or defends
2. Relatives
3. Calculating; plotting
4. Delay; get in the way of
5. Lessening; going away; ending
6. In command of magic, spells and witchcraft
7. Deep hatred
8. Top; high point
9. Payment
10. Thinking something exists, especially something wrong, without any proof
11. Corrected; made better
12. Journey undertaken with a definite objective
13. Words written in ancient Germanic letters
14. Long, loose-fitting shirt or coat
15. Ridiculous
16. Unavoidable

A=	B=	C=	D=
E=	F=	G=	H=
I=	J=	K=	L=
M=	N=	O=	P=

The Hobbit Vocabulary Magic Squares 4 Answer Key

Match the definition with the vocabulary word. Put your answers in the magic squares below. When your answers are correct, all columns and rows will add to the same number.

A. EXPEDITION
B. RUNES
C. GUARDIAN
D. PINNACLE
E. SORCEROUS
F. WILY
G. ABSURD
H. SUSPICION
I. ENMITY
J. KIN
K. TUNIC
L. AMENDED
M. REMUNERATION
N. INEVITABLE
O. HINDER
P. WANING

1. One who guards, protects or defends
2. Relatives
3. Calculating; plotting
4. Delay; get in the way of
5. Lessening; going away; ending
6. In command of magic, spells and witchcraft
7. Deep hatred
8. Top; high point
9. Payment
10. Thinking something exists, especially something wrong, without any proof
11. Corrected; made better
12. Journey undertaken with a definite objective
13. Words written in ancient Germanic letters
14. Long, loose-fitting shirt or coat
15. Ridiculous
16. Unavoidable

A=12	B=13	C=1	D=8
E=6	F=3	G=15	H=10
I=7	J=2	K=14	L=11
M=9	N=16	O=4	P=5

The Hobbit Vocabulary Word Search 1

Words are placed backwards, forward, diagonally, up and down. Clues listed below can help you find the words. Circle the hidden vocabulary words in the maze.

```
R E Q U I S I T E M A R A U D I N G C
O Z H U K S U O R E C R O S V T X G L
T R O X E N A I D R A U G N E V T Z M
A W I V I S P K C B B U S T L E H C R
R P S C L R T L K G S P R E C I S E Z
I Q T R A H S X U F U F K N A H M Z Y
P D U B I O U S D N R K O I N U B L B
S S N A E S O P E R D I B E N M I T Y
N T C N Y D L Z Z E T E K E I W N S L
O S A C S R I T D I T M R G P Y E U L
C H N E H M R N D D T A W N L P V S A
H I N D E R E E N B T T H G I L P I P U
S U Y N X M P M J I B B T R D D T I T
R R I D A X B L O P R E F E R R A C E
L A R D E R S N U I R H Z T A O B I P
V N F L Y L K P P R I D S O U L O R
Z S L E R O L P M I E S J U H G E N E
Q O H S I R E P L S M F R M Y H Q M P
W M T D E H S I N O T S A H R T P H T
```

A gathered, hidden, or stored supply or treasure (5)
Ask or beg urgently (7)
Calculating; plotting (4)
Commotion; hurried activity (6)
Continuously; always (11)
Corrected; made better (7)
Dangerous (8)
Deep hatred (6)
Delay; get in the way of (6)
Die; pass from existence (6)
Doubtful (7)
Entice; attract (4)
Exact (7)
Gathering (9)
Grabbed (6)
In command of magic, spells and witchcraft (9)
Journey undertaken with a definite objective (10)
Lacking substance; hollow; fruitless (4)
Lift up (5)
Long period of time with no rain (7)
Long, loose-fitting shirt or coat (5)
Male deer (4)
Narrative of experiences an author has lived through (7)
Nest built on a high place (5)

One who guards, protects or defends (8)
One who joins in planning or plotting (11)
Pantry or cupboards containing food stores (7)
Payment (12)
Relatives (3)
Release, give up or free in return for payment (6)
Required, necessary (9)
Rest (6)
Ridiculous (6)
Search (5)
Situation of difficulty (6)
Small, secluded, wooded valley (4)
Stolen property (7)
Surprised (10)
Thinking something exists, especially something wrong, without any proof (9)
To like better; rather (6)
Top; high point (8)
Unavoidable (10)
Unexplainable and strange, exciting wonder and fear (7)
Wandering in search of something to steal (9)
Wharf of reinforced bank where ships are loaded (4)
Words written in ancient Germanic letters (5)

The Hobbit Vocabulary Word Search 1 Answer Key

Words are placed backwards, forward, diagonally, up and down. Clues listed below can help you find the words. Circle the hidden vocabulary words in the maze.

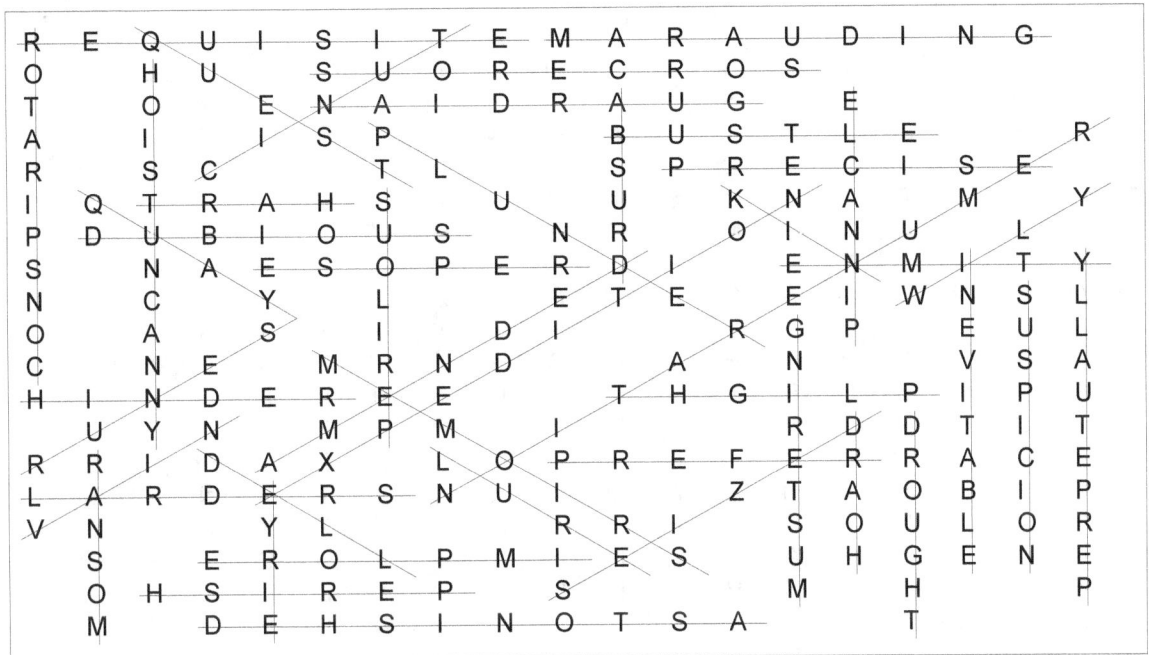

A gathered, hidden, or stored supply or treasure (5)
Ask or beg urgently (7)
Calculating; plotting (4)
Commotion; hurried activity (6)
Continuously; always (11)
Corrected; made better (7)
Dangerous (8)
Deep hatred (6)
Delay; get in the way of (6)
Die; pass from existence (6)
Doubtful (7)
Entice; attract (4)
Exact (7)
Gathering (9)
Grabbed (6)
In command of magic, spells and witchcraft (9)
Journey undertaken with a definite objective (10)
Lacking substance; hollow; fruitless (4)
Lift up (5)
Long period of time with no rain (7)
Long, loose-fitting shirt or coat (5)
Male deer (4)
Narrative of experiences an author has lived through (7)
Nest built on a high place (5)

One who guards, protects or defends (8)
One who joins in planning or plotting (11)
Pantry or cupboards containing food stores (7)
Payment (12)
Relatives (3)
Release, give up or free in return for payment (6)
Required, necessary (9)
Rest (6)
Ridiculous (6)
Search (5)
Situation of difficulty (6)
Small, secluded, wooded valley (4)
Stolen property (7)
Surprised (10)
Thinking something exists, especially something wrong, without any proof (9)
To like better; rather (6)
Top; high point (8)
Unavoidable (10)
Unexplainable and strange, exciting wonder and fear (7)
Wandering in search of something to steal (9)
Wharf of reinforced bank where ships are loaded (4)
Words written in ancient Germanic letters (5)

The Hobbit Vocabulary Word Search 2

Words are placed backwards, forward, diagonally, up and down. Clues listed below can help you find the words. Circle the hidden vocabulary words in the maze.

```
S E X P E D I T I O N A U N C A N N Y
E F P U M Y W U P Y O U A A Q P I J T
N Y R R O W R N W P I D M I U G M Z I
U Z E S V W I S A C A E D A V P L U U
R C C U H M P C E S I C N R Y V L H Q
E B I I T K E Z S T P I D A B E O S I
M A S N A R R M M O S O E U D A R Q T
U B E G O Y I O O N U U D G R E E F N
N O D M L M S S P I S Z D D E T W A A
E M L I L N H I F S R L Y R T Y A P H
R I W R A M N R Y H C S A I C N I L S
A N F R E N P Y T E J L S H I R R U O
T A D Q A P Y N I D W I R N E B U N R
I B G C X D O W M V U M G D L R F D C
O L L Z B H H S N Q A K N Z T X N E E
N E L B A H C A E P M I N U S Y I R R
P R E F E R A R R H H N N V U D N O
S E I Z E D T R P L I G H T B L C Y U
D R O U G H T L T S I O H Q U E S T S
```

A gathered, hidden, or stored supply or treasure (5)
Ask or beg urgently (7)
Beyond all doubt; unquestionable (13)
Calculating; plotting (4)
Chasing (8)
Commotion; hurried activity (6)
Corrected; made better (7)
Daring; bold (9)
Deep hatred (6)
Delay; get in the way of (6)
Die; pass from existence (6)
Entice; attract (4)
Exact (7)
Grabbed (6)
In command of magic, spells and witchcraft (9)
Journey undertaken with a definite objective (10)
Lacking substance; hollow; fruitless (4)
Lessening; going away; ending (6)
Lift up (5)
Long period of time with no rain (7)
Long, loose-fitting shirt or coat (5)
Male deer (4)
Narrative of experiences an author has lived through (7)
Nest built on a high place (5)

One who guards, protects or defends (8)
Pantry or cupboards containing food stores (7)
Payment (12)
Quality of being very old or ancient (9)
Relatives (3)
Release, give up or free in return for payment (6)
Repulsive; disgusting (9)
Required, necessary (9)
Rest (6)
Search (5)
Situation of difficulty (6)
Small, secluded, wooded valley (4)
Stolen property (7)
Surprised (10)
Thinking something exists, especially something wrong, without any proof (9)
Thoroughly unpleasant (10)
To like better; rather (6)
To make angry; enrage (9)
Top; high point (8)
Unexplainable and strange, exciting wonder and fear (7)
Wharf of reinforced bank where ships are loaded (4)
Words written in ancient Germanic letters (5)

The Hobbit Vocabulary Word Search 2 Answer Key

Words are placed backwards, forward, diagonally, up and down. Clues listed below can help you find the words. Circle the hidden vocabulary words in the maze.

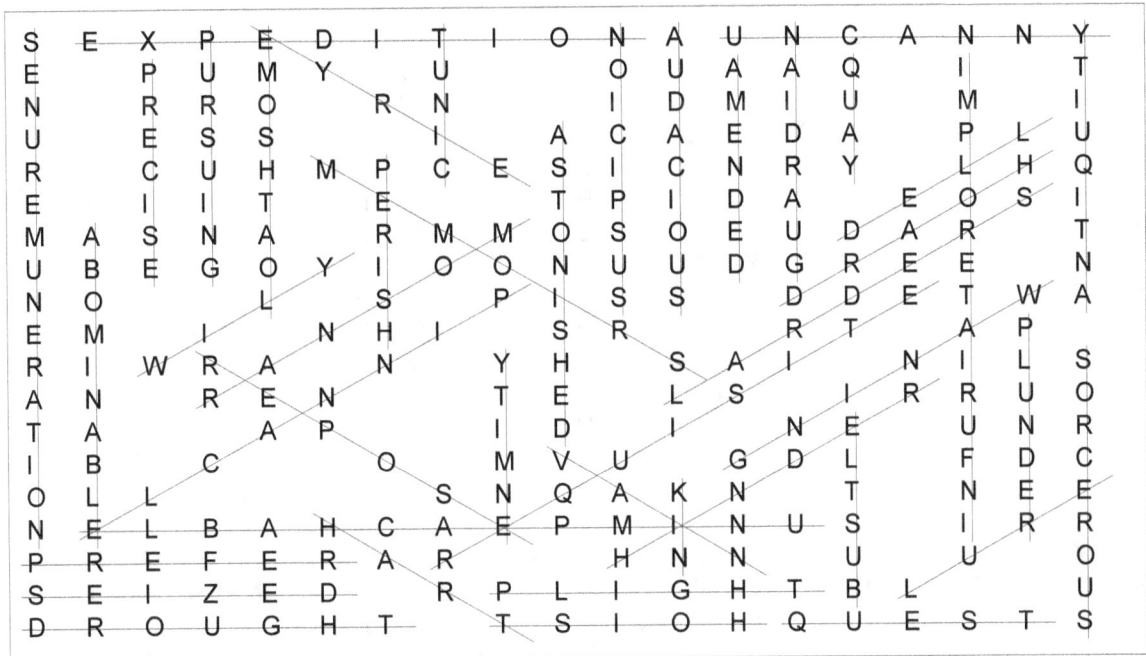

A gathered, hidden, or stored supply or treasure (5)
Ask or beg urgently (7)
Beyond all doubt; unquestionable (13)
Calculating; plotting (4)
Chasing (8)
Commotion; hurried activity (6)
Corrected; made better (7)
Daring; bold (9)
Deep hatred (6)
Delay; get in the way of (6)
Die; pass from existence (6)
Entice; attract (4)
Exact (7)
Grabbed (6)
In command of magic, spells and witchcraft (9)
Journey undertaken with a definite objective (10)
Lacking substance; hollow; fruitless (4)
Lessening; going away; ending (6)
Lift up (5)
Long period of time with no rain (7)
Long, loose-fitting shirt or coat (5)
Male deer (4)
Narrative of experiences an author has lived through (7)
Nest built on a high place (5)

One who guards, protects or defends (8)
Pantry or cupboards containing food stores (7)
Payment (12)
Quality of being very old or ancient (9)
Relatives (3)
Release, give up or free in return for payment (6)
Repulsive; disgusting (9)
Required, necessary (9)
Rest (6)
Search (5)
Situation of difficulty (6)
Small, secluded, wooded valley (4)
Stolen property (7)
Surprised (10)
Thinking something exists, especially something wrong, without any proof (9)
Thoroughly unpleasant (10)
To like better; rather (6)
To make angry; enrage (9)
Top; high point (8)
Unexplainable and strange, exciting wonder and fear (7)
Wharf of reinforced bank where ships are loaded (4)
Words written in ancient Germanic letters (5)

The Hobbit Vocabulary Word Search 3

Words are placed backwards, forward, diagonally, up and down. Words listed below are included in the maze. Circle the hidden vocabulary words in the maze.

```
P E R I L O U S U O I C A D U A L U R E
A I X N A I D R A U G I R W A N I N G Y
B E N M F R N B E V D N Y W S V K I T S
O X G N I U S R U P T U Z F T H Q M G H
M P N H A U L T H R O T V H O R C P D H
I E N F R C G C A L B S G G N L L E D D
N D O D E Q L H I C U I E N I Y M A N P
A I I E D U Q E M S L H O I S T F C N W
B T T D N E Z K P P G A K Y H I L H T F
L I A N I S L I E V N W R D E M O A I T
E O R E H T C L N J I X P D D N A B Q V
Z N E M S I W T T E R D Y K E E E T L U Y
V B N A O W H Y T B U S T L E R H E I N
L K U N X G X W R S A R E Q U I S I T E
X L M P U J R X A L R C H B V E O Q Y T
M C E O R S P N B Y A K N O I M M U R K
E Y R I E E R O L P M I R Z A D E A S C
M D X B R N C I E L A N E M W R N Y M G
B F Q I H U W I F V W D K N Z S D J V L
D C S T Y R R K S R K M E M O I R S D H
B H W P J G N I R E T S U M P R E F E R
```

ABOMINABLE	EYRIE	MARAUDING	RANSOM
ABSURD	GUARDIAN	MEMOIRS	REMUNERATION
AMENDED	HART	MUSTERING	REPOSE
ANTIQUITY	HINDER	PERILOUS	REQUISITE
ASTONISHED	HOARD	PERISH	RUNES
AUDACIOUS	HOIST	PINNACLE	SEIZED
BUSTLE	IMPENETRABLE	PLIGHT	SUSPICION
DELL	IMPLORE	PRECISE	TUNIC
DROUGHT	KIN	PREFER	UNIMPEACHABLE
EDDYING	LARDERS	PURSUING	VAIN
ENMITY	LOATHSOME	QUAY	WANING
EXPEDITION	LURE	QUEST	WILY

The Hobbit Vocabulary Word Search 3 Answer Key

Words are placed backwards, forward, diagonally, up and down. Words listed below are included in the maze. Circle the hidden vocabulary words in the maze.

```
P  E  R  I  L  O  U  S  U  O  I  C  A  D  U  A  L  U  R  E
A  I     N  A  I  D  R  A  U  G  I     W  A  N  I  N  G
B  E  N           B  E        N        S           I
O  X  G  N  I  U  S  R  U  P  T  U     T           M
M  P        A  U           R  O  T     H  O        P
   E  N     R  C           A           S  G  N  L  L  E  D
   D  O  D  E  Q  L  H  I        U  I  E  N  I  Y  A  A
   I  I  E  D  U     E  M  S     L  H  O  I  S  T  C  N
   T  T  D  N  E        P  P  G  A     Y  H  I  L  H  T
   I  A  N  I  S        E     N     R  D  E  M  O  A  I
E  O  R  E  H  T  C     N     I     D  D  N  A  B  L  Q
   N  E  M        I     E     D     E  E  E  T  L  U
         N  A  O     H     T  B  U  S  T  L  E  R  H  E
            U           G     R  A  R  E  Q  U  I  S  I  T  E
            M  P  U           A     R  H        E  O  Q  Y
            E  O  R  S  P     B  Y  A  K  N  O  I     M  U  R
E  Y  R  I  E  E  R  O  L  P  M  I        Z  A        E  A
   D        R  N  C  I  E     A  N  E              R  N  Y
               I  U  W  I     V     D              S  D
            S           R  S           M  E  M  O  I  R  S
      H              G  N  I  R  E  T  S  U  M  P  R  E  F  E  R
```

ABOMINABLE	EYRIE	MARAUDING	RANSOM
ABSURD	GUARDIAN	MEMOIRS	REMUNERATION
AMENDED	HART	MUSTERING	REPOSE
ANTIQUITY	HINDER	PERILOUS	REQUISITE
ASTONISHED	HOARD	PERISH	RUNES
AUDACIOUS	HOIST	PINNACLE	SEIZED
BUSTLE	IMPENETRABLE	PLIGHT	SUSPICION
DELL	IMPLORE	PRECISE	TUNIC
DROUGHT	KIN	PREFER	UNIMPEACHABLE
EDDYING	LARDERS	PURSUING	VAIN
ENMITY	LOATHSOME	QUAY	WANING
EXPEDITION	LURE	QUEST	WILY

The Hobbit Vocabulary Word Search 4

Words are placed backwards, forward, diagonally, up and down. Words listed below are included in the maze. Circle the hidden vocabulary words in the maze.

```
P P R E F E R P W R O U G H T Y K U G B
U R D R B M M L P Y Z H Z S T K X N B V
R E R O D K E U L Q R J L U S C C I Y Q
S Q O L G L S N I E U W N O N R N M K L
U U U P P A I D G D N Q D I Q H T P M K
I I G M L R C E H D E H U C V S O E T W
N S H I N D E R T Y S G U A R D I A N W
G I T B E E R M T I Z H M D Y S B C R K
G T H Z L R P I R N A E J U Y S Z H L D
Z E I T F S M E V G N Y A U W E A U W
P E S D R N P X F D N H T R E I L B R K
S U E E E S R J E E U R D I M L B L E D
B M S L V O W D L H C B R T Q Y A E F X
S U O L I R E P C S C Y I T Z U N Q W V
X S P F M C H Y A I E W R O S J I V F Y
Q T E P E E P J N N K A A M U H M T T D
P E R R M R F U N N O H V O N L S O N Y P
Z R Q D O O T Q I T H S I N I L B I H B
C I K V I U T Q P S N K Q V T N A A S D
Z N P Y R S Z E T A I R U F N I G V Z T
L G D T S E U Q R U N C A N N Y L M Q D
```

ABOMINABLE	EYRIE	MUSTERING	REPOSE
ABSURD	GUARDIAN	PERILOUS	REQUISITE
AMENDED	HART	PERISH	RUNES
ANTIQUITY	HINDER	PINNACLE	SEIZED
ASTONISHED	HOARD	PLIGHT	SORCEROUS
AUDACIOUS	HOIST	PLUNDER	TUNIC
BUSTLE	IMPLORE	PRECISE	UNCANNY
DELL	INFURIATE	PREFER	UNIMPEACHABLE
DROUGHT	KIN	PURSUING	VAIN
DUBIOUS	LARDERS	QUAY	WANING
EDDYING	LURE	QUEST	WILY
ENMITY	MEMOIRS	RANSOM	WROUGHT

The Hobbit Vocabulary Word Search 4 Answer Key

Words are placed backwards, forward, diagonally, up and down. Words listed below are included in the maze. Circle the hidden vocabulary words in the maze.

ABOMINABLE	EYRIE	MUSTERING	REPOSE
ABSURD	GUARDIAN	PERILOUS	REQUISITE
AMENDED	HART	PERISH	RUNES
ANTIQUITY	HINDER	PINNACLE	SEIZED
ASTONISHED	HOARD	PLIGHT	SORCEROUS
AUDACIOUS	HOIST	PLUNDER	TUNIC
BUSTLE	IMPLORE	PRECISE	UNCANNY
DELL	INFURIATE	PREFER	UNIMPEACHABLE
DROUGHT	KIN	PURSUING	VAIN
DUBIOUS	LARDERS	QUAY	WANING
EDDYING	LURE	QUEST	WILY
ENMITY	MEMOIRS	RANSOM	WROUGHT

The Hobbit Vocabulary Crossword 1

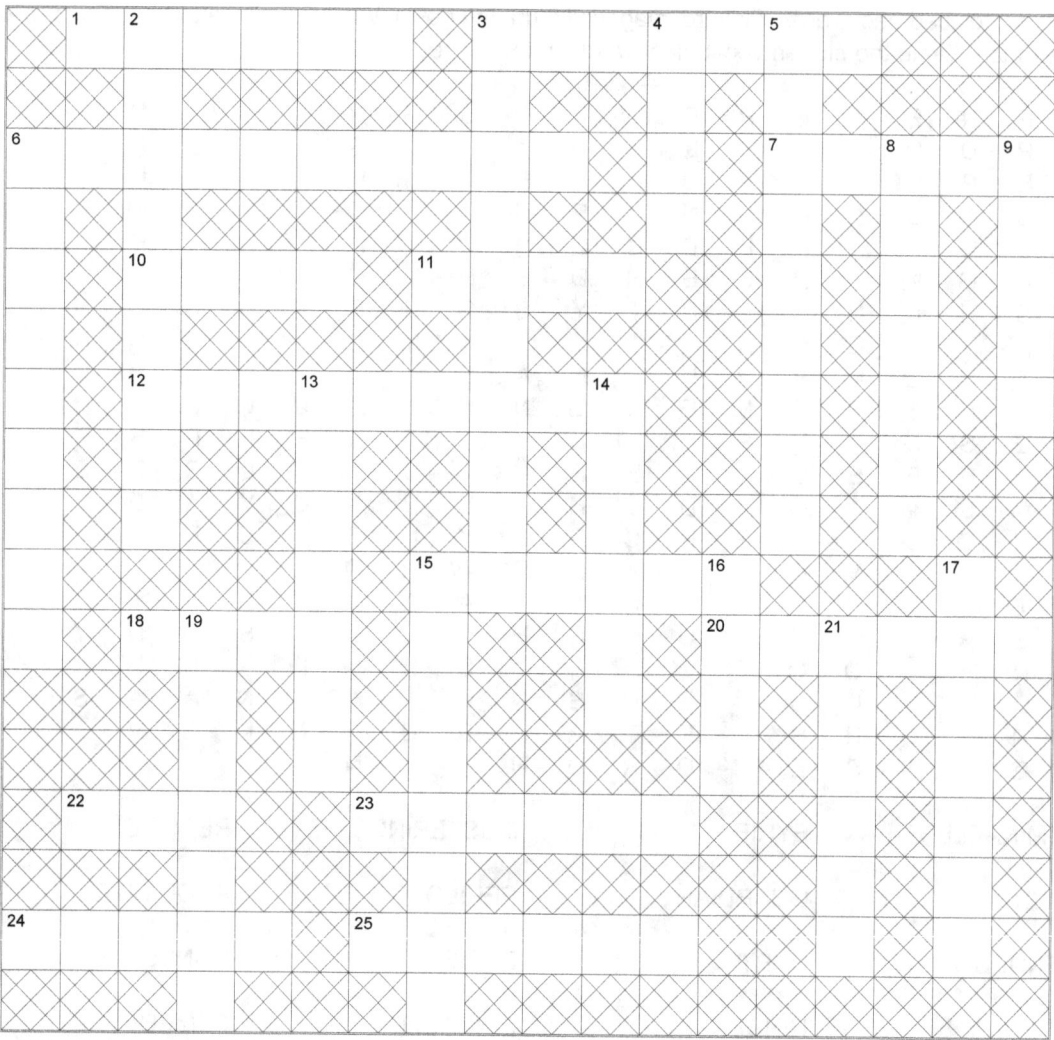

Across
1. Release, give up or free in return for payment
3. Ask or beg urgently
6. Surprised
7. Search
10. Wharf of reinforced bank where ships are loaded
11. Calculating; plotting
12. To make angry; enrage
15. Die; pass from existence
18. Lacking substance; hollow; fruitless
20. Ridiculous
22. Relatives
23. Situation of difficulty
24. Words written in ancient Germanic letters
25. Commotion; hurried activity

Down
2. Quality of being very old or ancient
3. Unavoidable
4. Entice; attract
5. Required, necessary
6. Daring; bold
8. Going against the main current, especially in a swirling motion
9. Long, loose-fitting shirt or coat
13. Unexplainable and strange, exciting wonder and fear
14. Deep hatred
15. Dangerous
16. Male deer
17. Shaped; worked
19. Corrected; made better
21. Grabbed

The Hobbit Vocabulary Crossword 1 Answer Key

Across
1. Release, give up or free in return for payment
3. Ask or beg urgently
6. Surprised
7. Search
10. Wharf of reinforced bank where ships are loaded
11. Calculating; plotting
12. To make angry; enrage
15. Die; pass from existence
18. Lacking substance; hollow; fruitless
20. Ridiculous
22. Relatives
23. Situation of difficulty
24. Words written in ancient Germanic letters
25. Commotion; hurried activity

Down
2. Quality of being very old or ancient
3. Unavoidable
4. Entice; attract
5. Required, necessary
6. Daring; bold
8. Going against the main current, especially in a swirling motion
9. Long, loose-fitting shirt or coat
13. Unexplainable and strange, exciting wonder and fear
14. Deep hatred
15. Dangerous
16. Male deer
17. Shaped; worked
19. Corrected; made better
21. Grabbed

The Hobbit Vocabulary Crossword 2

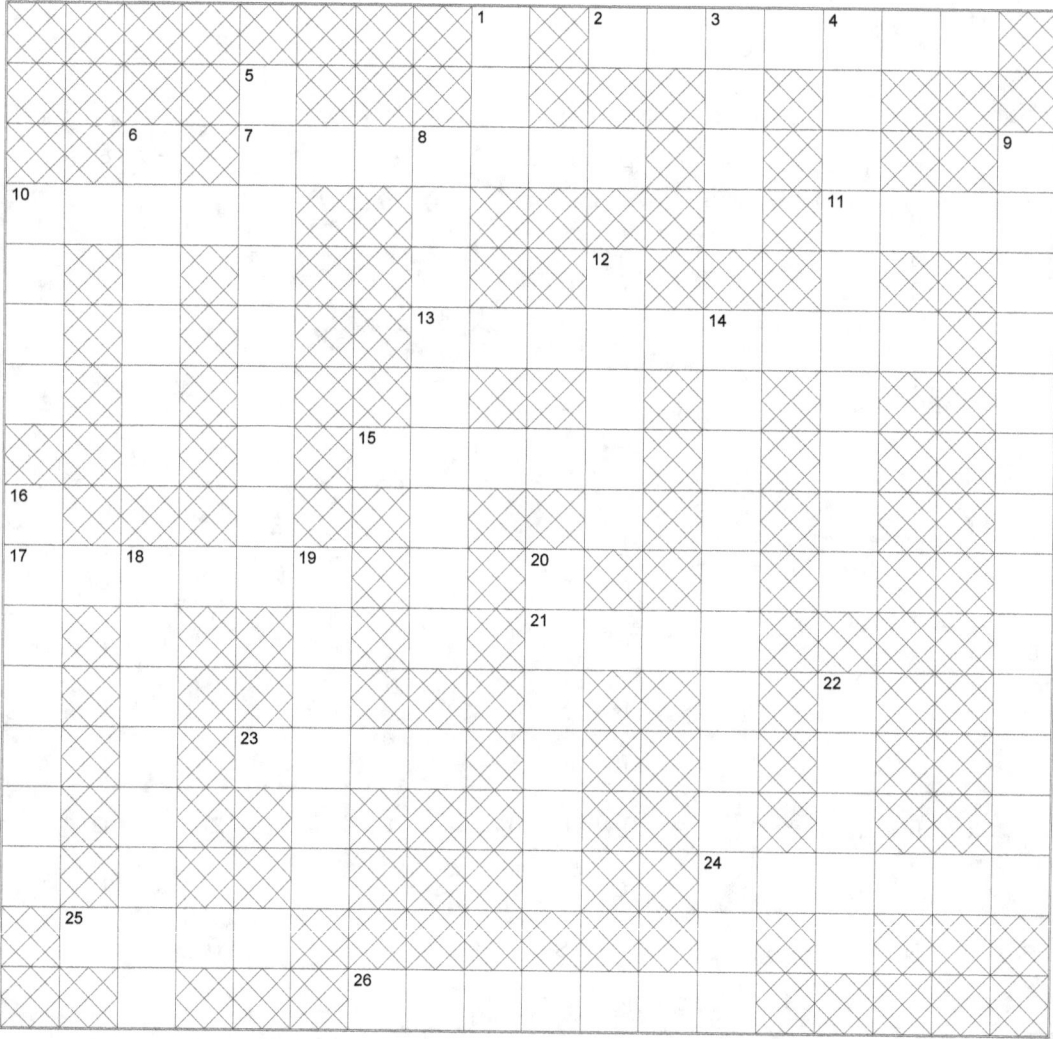

Across
2. Going against the main current, especially in a swirling motion
7. Unexplainable and strange, exciting wonder and fear
10. A gathered, hidden, or stored supply or treasure
11. Lacking substance; hollow; fruitless
13. To make angry; enrage
15. Words written in ancient Germanic letters
17. Rest
21. Entice; attract
23. Calculating; plotting
24. Commotion; hurried activity
25. Wharf of reinforced bank where ships are loaded
26. Ask or beg urgently

Down
1. Relatives
3. Small, secluded, wooded valley
4. Unavoidable
5. Daring; bold
6. Release, give up or free in return for payment
8. Quality of being very old or ancient
9. Beyond all doubt; unquestionable
10. Male deer
12. Search
14. Can't be pierced or entered through
16. Shaped; worked
18. Dangerous
19. Deep hatred
20. Situation of difficulty
22. Lift up

The Hobbit Vocabulary Crossword 2 Answer Key

Across
2. Going against the main current, especially in a swirling motion
7. Unexplainable and strange, exciting wonder and fear
10. A gathered, hidden, or stored supply or treasure
11. Lacking substance; hollow; fruitless
13. To make angry; enrage
15. Words written in ancient Germanic letters
17. Rest
21. Entice; attract
23. Calculating; plotting
24. Commotion; hurried activity
25. Wharf of reinforced bank where ships are loaded
26. Ask or beg urgently

Down
1. Relatives
3. Small, secluded, wooded valley
4. Unavoidable
5. Daring; bold
6. Release, give up or free in return for payment
8. Quality of being very old or ancient
9. Beyond all doubt; unquestionable
10. Male deer
12. Search
14. Can't be pierced or entered through
16. Shaped; worked
18. Dangerous
19. Deep hatred
20. Situation of difficulty
22. Lift up

The Hobbit Vocabulary Crossword 3

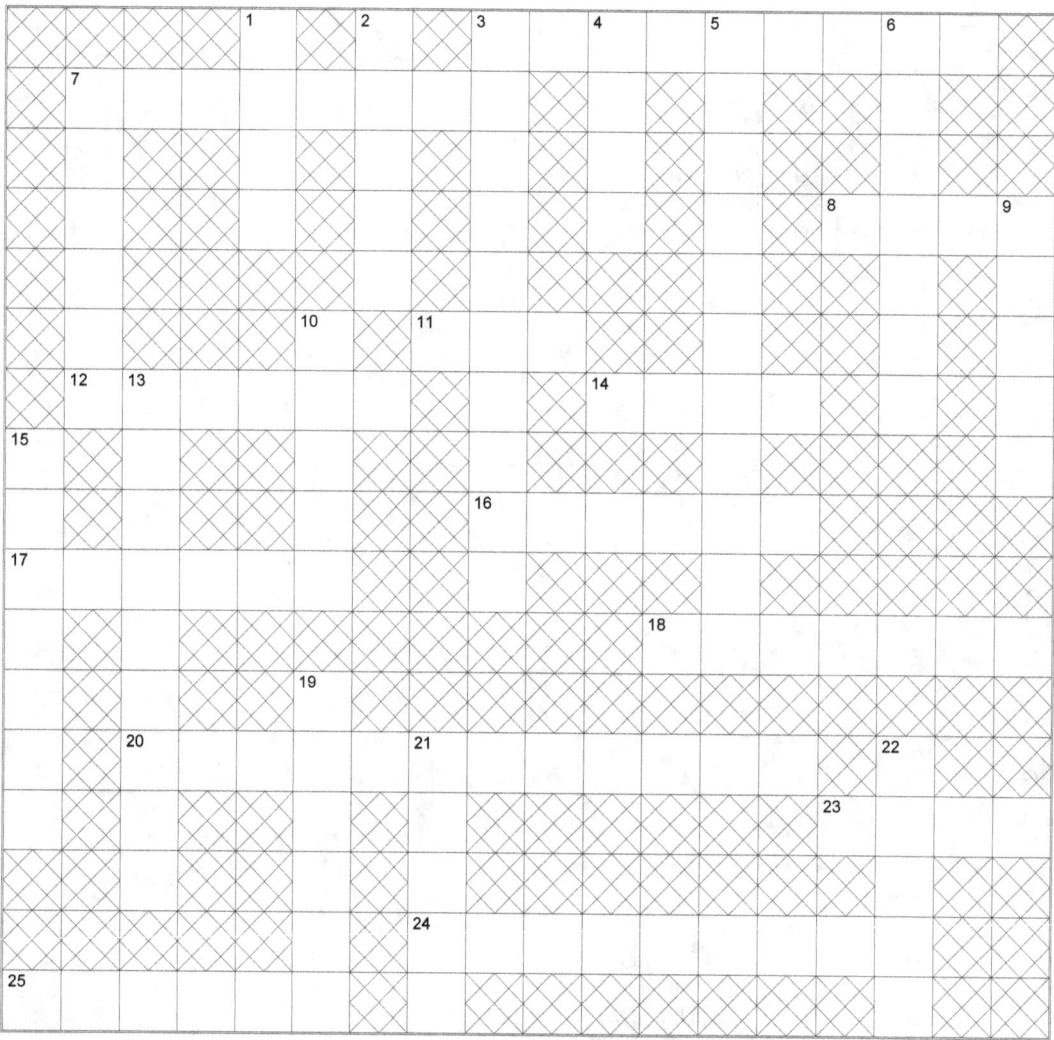

Across
3. Daring; bold
7. Dangerous
8. Male deer
11. Relatives
12. Release, give up or free in return for payment
14. Entice; attract
16. Deep hatred
17. Situation of difficulty
18. Shaped; worked
20. Can't be pierced or entered through
23. Wharf of reinforced bank where ships are loaded
24. To make angry; enrage
25. Commotion; hurried activity

Down
1. Calculating; plotting
2. A gathered, hidden, or stored supply or treasure
3. Surprised
4. Small, secluded, wooded valley
5. One who joins in planning or plotting
6. Unexplainable and strange, exciting wonder and fear
7. To like better; rather
9. Long, loose-fitting shirt or coat
10. Lift up
13. Quality of being very old or ancient
15. Ask or beg urgently
19. Rest
21. Nest built on a high place
22. Words written in ancient Germanic letters

The Hobbit Vocabulary Crossword 3 Answer Key

Across
- 3. Daring; bold
- 7. Dangerous
- 8. Male deer
- 11. Relatives
- 12. Release, give up or free in return for payment
- 14. Entice; attract
- 16. Deep hatred
- 17. Situation of difficulty
- 18. Shaped; worked
- 20. Can't be pierced or entered through
- 23. Wharf of reinforced bank where ships are loaded
- 24. To make angry; enrage
- 25. Commotion; hurried activity

Down
- 1. Calculating; plotting
- 2. A gathered, hidden, or stored supply or treasure
- 3. Surprised
- 4. Small, secluded, wooded valley
- 5. One who joins in planning or plotting
- 6. Unexplainable and strange, exciting wonder and fear
- 7. To like better; rather
- 9. Long, loose-fitting shirt or coat
- 10. Lift up
- 13. Quality of being very old or ancient
- 15. Ask or beg urgently
- 19. Rest
- 21. Nest built on a high place
- 22. Words written in ancient Germanic letters

The Hobbit Vocabulary Crossword 4

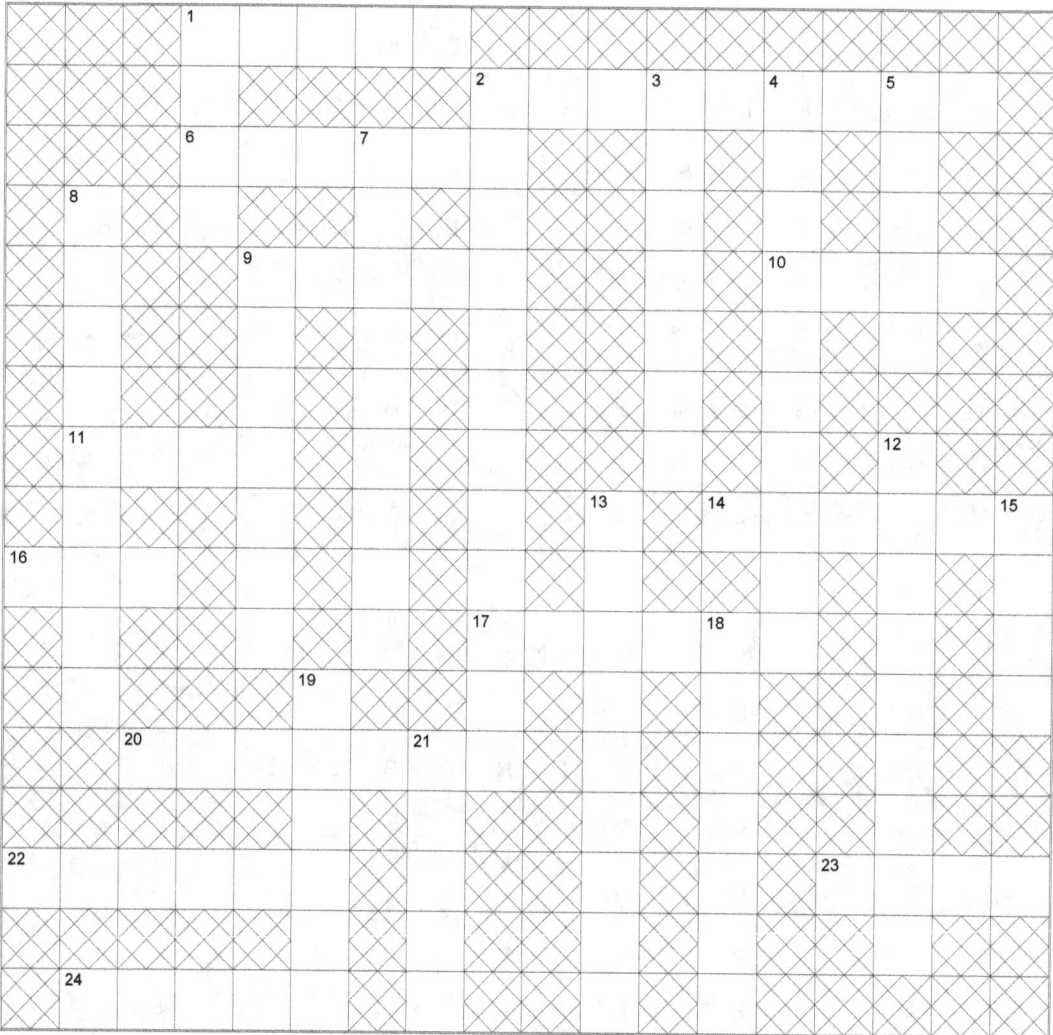

Across
1. A gathered, hidden, or stored supply or treasure
2. To make angry; enrage
6. Release, give up or free in return for payment
9. Nest built on a high place
10. Lacking substance; hollow; fruitless
11. Wharf of reinforced bank where ships are loaded
14. Ridiculous
16. Relatives
17. Commotion; hurried activity
20. Ask or beg urgently
22. Lessening; going away; ending
23. Entice; attract
24. Search

Down
1. Male deer
2. Can't be pierced or entered through
3. Unexplainable and strange, exciting wonder and fear
4. Unavoidable
5. Long, loose-fitting shirt or coat
7. In command of magic, spells and witchcraft
8. Quality of being very old or ancient
9. Going against the main current, especially in a swirling motion
12. Daring; bold
13. Gathering
15. Small, secluded, wooded valley
18. Pantry or cupboards containing food stores
19. Situation of difficulty
21. Words written in ancient Germanic letters

The Hobbit Vocabulary Crossword 4 Answer Key

			1 H	O	A	R	D							
			A				2 I	N	F	3 U	R	4 I	A	5 T	E
		6 R	A	N	7 S	O	M			N		N		U	
8 A		T			O		P			C		E		N	
N			9 E	Y	R	I	E			A		10 V	A	I	N
T			D		C		N			N		I		C	
I			D		E		E			N		T			
11 Q	U	A	Y		R		T			Y		A		12 A	
U				I		O		R		13 M	14 A	B	S	U	R	15 D
16 K	I	N		N		U		A		U		L		D		E
T			G		S		17 B	U	S	T	18 L	E		A		L
Y				19 P		L		T			A			C		L
	20 I	M	P	L	O	21 R	E			E		R		I	
			I		U				R		D		O	
22 W	A	N	I	N	G		N			I		E		23 L	U	R	E
			H		E				N		R		S	
	24 Q	U	E	S	T		S			G		S		

Across
1. A gathered, hidden, or stored supply or treasure
2. To make angry; enrage
6. Release, give up or free in return for payment
9. Nest built on a high place
10. Lacking substance; hollow; fruitless
11. Wharf of reinforced bank where ships are loaded
14. Ridiculous
16. Relatives
17. Commotion; hurried activity
20. Ask or beg urgently
22. Lessening; going away; ending
23. Entice; attract
24. Search

Down
1. Male deer
2. Can't be pierced or entered through
3. Unexplainable and strange, exciting wonder and fear
4. Unavoidable
5. Long, loose-fitting shirt or coat
7. In command of magic, spells and witchcraft
8. Quality of being very old or ancient
9. Going against the main current, especially in a swirling motion
12. Daring; bold
13. Gathering
15. Small, secluded, wooded valley
18. Pantry or cupboards containing food stores
19. Situation of difficulty
21. Words written in ancient Germanic letters

The Hobbit Vocabulary Juggle Letters 1

1. NPRCTIRAOSO = 1. _____
   One who joins in planning or plotting

2. IENHRD = 2. _____
   Delay; get in the way of

3. TORUEINAMNRE = 3. _____
   Payment

4. PIEBTERELMAN = 4. _____
   Can't be pierced or entered through

5. IUSLPEOR = 5. _____
   Dangerous

6. LENTAIVBEI = 6. _____
   Unavoidable

7. BBMAIEONLA = 7. _____
   Thoroughly unpleasant

8. NNCAYNU = 8. _____
   Unexplainable and strange, exciting wonder and fear

9. OOHTASLEM = 9. _____
   Repulsive; disgusting

10. ELBUTS =10. _____
    Commotion; hurried activity

11. TIOSH =11. _____
    Lift up

12. OTNDEPIXIE =12. _____
    Journey undertaken with a definite objective

13. SNITREMGU =13. _____
    Gathering

14. NHITDSOSAE =14. _____
    Surprised

15. REYIE =15. _____
    Nest built on a high place

The Hobbit Vocabulary Juggle Letters 1 Answer Key

1. NPRCTIRAOSO = 1. CONSPIRATOR
   One who joins in planning or plotting

2. IENHRD = 2. HINDER
   Delay; get in the way of

3. TORUEINAMNRE = 3. REMUNERATION
   Payment

4. PIEBTERELMAN = 4. IMPENETRABLE
   Can't be pierced or entered through

5. IUSLPEOR = 5. PERILOUS
   Dangerous

6. LENTAIVBEI = 6. INEVITABLE
   Unavoidable

7. BBMAIEONLA = 7. ABOMINABLE
   Thoroughly unpleasant

8. NNCAYNU = 8. UNCANNY
   Unexplainable and strange, exciting wonder and fear

9. OOHTASLEM = 9. LOATHSOME
   Repulsive; disgusting

10. ELBUTS = 10. BUSTLE
    Commotion; hurried activity

11. TIOSH = 11. HOIST
    Lift up

12. OTNDEPIXIE = 12. EXPEDITION
    Journey undertaken with a definite objective

13. SNITREMGU = 13. MUSTERING
    Gathering

14. NHITDSOSAE = 14. ASTONISHED
    Surprised

15. REYIE = 15. EYRIE
    Nest built on a high place

The Hobbit Vocabulary Juggle Letters 2

1. ESTQU = 1. _____
Search

2. PILERMO = 2. _____
Ask or beg urgently

3. SIONEADHST = 3. _____
Surprised

4. TAFUEINRI = 4. _____
To make angry; enrage

5. EDLL = 5. _____
Small, secluded, wooded valley

6. CIANEPNL = 6. _____
Top; high point

7. TAOCNIOSPRR = 7. _____
One who joins in planning or plotting

8. DUBUIOS = 8. _____
Doubtful

9. SIOCIUSNP = 9. _____
Thinking something exists, especially something wrong, without any proof

10. RNSEU = 10. _____
Words written in ancient Germanic letters

11. EERRFP = 11. _____
To like better; rather

12. UNPLDRE = 12. _____
Stolen property

13. DYIGDNE = 13. _____
Going against the main current, especially in a swirling motion

14. ROEMSIM = 14. _____
Narrative of experiences an author has lived through

15. URORSOESC = 15. _____
In command of magic, spells and witchcraft

The Hobbit Vocabulary Juggle Letters 2 Answer Key

1. ESTQU = 1. QUEST
Search

2. PILERMO = 2. IMPLORE
Ask or beg urgently

3. SIONEADHST = 3. ASTONISHED
Surprised

4. TAFUEINRI = 4. INFURIATE
To make angry; enrage

5. EDLL = 5. DELL
Small, secluded, wooded valley

6. CIANEPNL = 6. PINNACLE
Top; high point

7. TAOCNIOSPRR = 7. CONSPIRATOR
One who joins in planning or plotting

8. DUBUIOS = 8. DUBIOUS
Doubtful

9. SIOCIUSNP = 9. SUSPICION
Thinking something exists, especially something wrong, without any proof

10. RNSEU = 10. RUNES
Words written in ancient Germanic letters

11. EERRFP = 11. PREFER
To like better; rather

12. UNPLDRE = 12. PLUNDER
Stolen property

13. DYIGDNE = 13. EDDYING
Going against the main current, especially in a swirling motion

14. ROEMSIM = 14. MEMOIRS
Narrative of experiences an author has lived through

15. URORSOESC = 15. SORCEROUS
In command of magic, spells and witchcraft

The Hobbit Vocabulary Juggle Letters 3

1. YLIW = 1. _____
   Calculating; plotting

2. NDDSREOPIAET = 2. _____
   Acts of preying upon others

3. LAENCNPI = 3. _____
   Top; high point

4. AIANGUDR = 4. _____
   One who guards, protects or defends

5. DHRUGOT = 5. _____
   Long period of time with no rain

6. HLTGPI = 6. _____
   Situation of difficulty

7. RLUE = 7. _____
   Entice; attract

8. LLDE = 8. _____
   Small, secluded, wooded valley

9. MIONELBABA = 9. _____
   Thoroughly unpleasant

10. PRUOSILE =10. _____
    Dangerous

11. NLPERDU =11. _____
    Stolen property

12. YNCANNU =12. _____
    Unexplainable and strange, exciting wonder and fear

13. IENEIPDXTO =13. _____
    Journey undertaken with a definite objective

14. IGYEDND =14. _____
    Going against the main current, especially in a swirling motion

15. IAUDCUASO =15. _____
    Daring; bold

The Hobbit Vocabulary Juggle Letters 3 Answer Key

1. YLIW = 1. WILY
Calculating; plotting

2. NDDSREOPIAET = 2. DEPREDATIONS
Acts of preying upon others

3. LAENCNPI = 3. PINNACLE
Top; high point

4. AIANGUDR = 4. GUARDIAN
One who guards, protects or defends

5. DHRUGOT = 5. DROUGHT
Long period of time with no rain

6. HLTGPI = 6. PLIGHT
Situation of difficulty

7. RLUE = 7. LURE
Entice; attract

8. LLDE = 8. DELL
Small, secluded, wooded valley

9. MIONELBABA = 9. ABOMINABLE
Thoroughly unpleasant

10. PRUOSILE = 10. PERILOUS
Dangerous

11. NLPERDU = 11. PLUNDER
Stolen property

12. YNCANNU = 12. UNCANNY
Unexplainable and strange, exciting wonder and fear

13. IENEIPDXTO = 13. EXPEDITION
Journey undertaken with a definite objective

14. IGYEDND = 14. EDDYING
Going against the main current, especially in a swirling motion

15. IAUDCUASO = 15. AUDACIOUS
Daring; bold

The Hobbit Vocabulary Juggle Letters 4

1. EHISRP = 1. _____
   Die; pass from existence

2. LBNERPEIMTEA = 2. _____
   Can't be pierced or entered through

3. NIK = 3. _____
   Relatives

4. YUNCNAN = 4. _____
   Unexplainable and strange, exciting wonder and fear

5. NAVI = 5. _____
   Lacking substance; hollow; fruitless

6. ROMMESI = 6. _____
   Narrative of experiences an author has lived through

7. MHCAUABLEPNIE = 7. _____
   Beyond all doubt; unquestionable

8. SLIEUROP = 8. _____
   Dangerous

9. NGANWI = 9. _____
   Lessening; going away; ending

10. ICUNT =10. _____
    Long, loose-fitting shirt or coat

11. SRNEU =11. _____
    Words written in ancient Germanic letters

12. YREEI =12. _____
    Nest built on a high place

13. SUOBIUD =13. _____
    Doubtful

14. ADMNEDE =14. _____
    Corrected; made better

15. EEXDPIOTNI =15. _____
    Journey undertaken with a definite objective

The Hobbit Vocabulary Juggle Letters 4 Answer Key

1. EHISRP = 1. PERISH
Die; pass from existence

2. LBNERPEIMTEA = 2. IMPENETRABLE
Can't be pierced or entered through

3. NIK = 3. KIN
Relatives

4. YUNCNAN = 4. UNCANNY
Unexplainable and strange, exciting wonder and fear

5. NAVI = 5. VAIN
Lacking substance; hollow; fruitless

6. ROMMESI = 6. MEMOIRS
Narrative of experiences an author has lived through

7. MHCAUABLEPNIE = 7. UNIMPEACHABLE
Beyond all doubt; unquestionable

8. SLIEUROP = 8. PERILOUS
Dangerous

9. NGANWI = 9. WANING
Lessening; going away; ending

10. ICUNT = 10. TUNIC
Long, loose-fitting shirt or coat

11. SRNEU = 11. RUNES
Words written in ancient Germanic letters

12. YREEI = 12. EYRIE
Nest built on a high place

13. SUOBIUD = 13. DUBIOUS
Doubtful

14. ADMNEDE = 14. AMENDED
Corrected; made better

15. EEXDPIOTNI = 15. EXPEDITION
Journey undertaken with a definite objective

ABOMINABLE	Thoroughly unpleasant
ABSURD	Ridiculous
AMENDED	Corrected; made better
ANTIQUITY	Quality of being very old or ancient
ASTONISHED	Surprised
AUDACIOUS	Daring; bold

BUSTLE	Commotion; hurried activity
CONSPIRATOR	One who joins in planning or plotting
DELL	Small, secluded, wooded valley
DEPREDATIONS	Acts of preying upon others
DROUGHT	Long period of time with no rain
DUBIOUS	Doubtful

EDDYING	Going against the main current, especially in a swirling motion
ENMITY	Deep hatred
EXPEDITION	Journey undertaken with a definite objective
EYRIE	Nest built on a high place
GUARDIAN	One who guards, protects or defends
HART	Male deer

HINDER	Delay; get in the way of
HOARD	A gathered, hidden, or stored supply or treasure
HOIST	Lift up
IMPENETRABLE	Can't be pierced or entered through
IMPLORE	Ask or beg urgently
INEVITABLE	Unavoidable

INFURIATE	To make angry; enrage
KIN	Relatives
LARDERS	Pantry or cupboards containing food stores
LOATHSOME	Repulsive; disgusting
LURE	Entice; attract
MARAUDING	Wandering in search of something to steal

MEMOIRS	Narrative of experiences an author has lived through
MUSTERING	Gathering
PERILOUS	Dangerous
PERISH	Die; pass from existence
PERPETUALLY	Continuously; always
PINNACLE	Top; high point

PLIGHT	Situation of difficulty
PLUNDER	Stolen property
PRECISE	Exact
PREFER	To like better; rather
PURSUING	Chasing
QUAY	Wharf of reinforced bank where ships are loaded

QUEST	Search
RANSOM	Release, give up or free in return for payment
REMUNERATION	Payment
REPOSE	Rest
REQUISITE	Required, necessary
RUNES	Words written in ancient Germanic letters

SEIZED	Grabbed
SORCEROUS	In command of magic, spells and witchcraft
SUSPICION	Thinking something exists, especially something wrong, without any proof
TUNIC	Long, loose-fitting shirt or coat
UNCANNY	Unexplainable and strange, exciting wonder and fear
UNIMPEACHABLE	Beyond all doubt; unquestionable

VAIN	Lacking substance; hollow; fruitless
WANING	Lessening; going away; ending
WILY	Calculating; plotting
WROUGHT	Shaped; worked

The Hobbit Vocabulary

EDDYING	DEPREDATIONS	PERISH	ANTIQUITY	ASTONISHED
VAIN	INEVITABLE	PREFER	PURSUING	DUBIOUS
EYRIE	REPOSE	FREE SPACE	MARAUDING	LURE
QUEST	SORCEROUS	HOIST	DELL	KIN
ABOMINABLE	SUSPICION	UNCANNY	ENMITY	HART

The Hobbit Vocabulary

MEMOIRS	MUSTERING	PLUNDER	AUDACIOUS	IMPLORE
INFURIATE	HOARD	WROUGHT	PLIGHT	UNIMPEACHABLE
GUARDIAN	WANING	FREE SPACE	REQUISITE	PERPETUALLY
BUSTLE	IMPENETRABLE	LOATHSOME	HINDER	RUNES
SEIZED	PERILOUS	DROUGHT	PINNACLE	AMENDED

The Hobbit Vocabulary

SEIZED	IMPLORE	PURSUING	EXPEDITION	WANING
QUAY	GUARDIAN	RANSOM	PINNACLE	DROUGHT
EYRIE	DUBIOUS	FREE SPACE	REPOSE	PERPETUALLY
PREFER	WROUGHT	AMENDED	IMPENETRABLE	ANTIQUITY
PERILOUS	ABOMINABLE	PLUNDER	ENMITY	LOATHSOME

The Hobbit Vocabulary

UNIMPEACHABLE	EDDYING	HART	SORCEROUS	QUEST
BUSTLE	TUNIC	MARAUDING	REMUNERATION	HOIST
DELL	MEMOIRS	FREE SPACE	CONSPIRATOR	VAIN
INEVITABLE	PLIGHT	REQUISITE	ASTONISHED	HOARD
MUSTERING	HINDER	DEPREDATIONS	INFURIATE	RUNES

The Hobbit Vocabulary

IMPENETRABLE	WILY	ASTONISHED	SEIZED	LURE
HOARD	TUNIC	MUSTERING	WANING	PLIGHT
LOATHSOME	HINDER	FREE SPACE	CONSPIRATOR	LARDERS
ANTIQUITY	EYRIE	PERISH	UNIMPEACHABLE	HART
DUBIOUS	PERILOUS	SORCEROUS	PERPETUALLY	BUSTLE

The Hobbit Vocabulary

DELL	SUSPICION	REPOSE	AUDACIOUS	KIN
VAIN	QUEST	ENMITY	MARAUDING	UNCANNY
ABSURD	EXPEDITION	FREE SPACE	QUAY	WROUGHT
GUARDIAN	PURSUING	RANSOM	ABOMINABLE	AMENDED
EDDYING	REMUNERATION	DEPREDATIONS	RUNES	PINNACLE

The Hobbit Vocabulary

BUSTLE	SEIZED	EXPEDITION	PLIGHT	MEMOIRS
AUDACIOUS	PERPETUALLY	LARDERS	HOARD	PERISH
LOATHSOME	ASTONISHED	FREE SPACE	MARAUDING	KIN
PRECISE	QUEST	GUARDIAN	PLUNDER	INFURIATE
WILY	PREFER	HART	MUSTERING	ABOMINABLE

The Hobbit Vocabulary

ANTIQUITY	IMPLORE	REPOSE	CONSPIRATOR	VAIN
TUNIC	EYRIE	DROUGHT	HOIST	DUBIOUS
QUAY	LURE	FREE SPACE	WANING	AMENDED
PERILOUS	INEVITABLE	PINNACLE	EDDYING	ENMITY
REQUISITE	UNCANNY	UNIMPEACHABLE	RANSOM	HINDER

The Hobbit Vocabulary

HART	WILY	QUAY	BUSTLE	IMPLORE
HINDER	PERISH	EYRIE	EXPEDITION	PLIGHT
RANSOM	AUDACIOUS	FREE SPACE	ABSURD	DEPREDATIONS
LARDERS	PLUNDER	EDDYING	DELL	DROUGHT
PERILOUS	DUBIOUS	REPOSE	LURE	ANTIQUITY

The Hobbit Vocabulary

QUEST	TUNIC	VAIN	INFURIATE	MEMOIRS
KIN	PERPETUALLY	MUSTERING	SEIZED	SORCEROUS
MARAUDING	ABOMINABLE	FREE SPACE	PRECISE	CONSPIRATOR
IMPENETRABLE	WROUGHT	REMUNERATION	REQUISITE	HOARD
LOATHSOME	PURSUING	PINNACLE	UNCANNY	HOIST

The Hobbit Vocabulary

EDDYING	WANING	INFURIATE	ABOMINABLE	REPOSE
MARAUDING	DROUGHT	GUARDIAN	IMPENETRABLE	PERPETUALLY
UNCANNY	HART	FREE SPACE	QUAY	AMENDED
BUSTLE	PREFER	DEPREDATIONS	WROUGHT	PERISH
RANSOM	SORCEROUS	EXPEDITION	REMUNERATION	PERILOUS

The Hobbit Vocabulary

UNIMPEACHABLE	LURE	PINNACLE	PLIGHT	ABSURD
PRECISE	VAIN	ANTIQUITY	ENMITY	SUSPICION
REQUISITE	PURSUING	FREE SPACE	HINDER	ASTONISHED
IMPLORE	HOIST	DELL	AUDACIOUS	MUSTERING
CONSPIRATOR	SEIZED	EYRIE	RUNES	QUEST

The Hobbit Vocabulary

PRECISE	REQUISITE	ASTONISHED	RANSOM	PINNACLE
VAIN	DUBIOUS	QUAY	PREFER	SEIZED
LARDERS	HART	FREE SPACE	INFURIATE	MARAUDING
TUNIC	HOARD	RUNES	ABSURD	DROUGHT
ENMITY	KIN	EYRIE	LURE	QUEST

The Hobbit Vocabulary

IMPLORE	DELL	ANTIQUITY	LOATHSOME	REMUNERATION
PERILOUS	AMENDED	PERISH	REPOSE	SORCEROUS
UNIMPEACHABLE	IMPENETRABLE	FREE SPACE	PLUNDER	PERPETUALLY
INEVITABLE	PURSUING	MUSTERING	SUSPICION	GUARDIAN
MEMOIRS	WANING	CONSPIRATOR	WILY	WROUGHT

The Hobbit Vocabulary

EXPEDITION	ANTIQUITY	EDDYING	REPOSE	LARDERS
TUNIC	RUNES	INEVITABLE	HOARD	UNIMPEACHABLE
GUARDIAN	PREFER	FREE SPACE	PERPETUALLY	PINNACLE
RANSOM	DUBIOUS	SEIZED	MEMOIRS	REQUISITE
HINDER	LOATHSOME	ENMITY	ABSURD	QUEST

The Hobbit Vocabulary

IMPLORE	PLIGHT	HART	REMUNERATION	WROUGHT
PRECISE	DEPREDATIONS	ABOMINABLE	VAIN	DELL
CONSPIRATOR	WANING	FREE SPACE	SUSPICION	PLUNDER
WILY	IMPENETRABLE	SORCEROUS	PERISH	PERILOUS
EYRIE	HOIST	INFURIATE	ASTONISHED	DROUGHT

The Hobbit Vocabulary

HOIST	PLIGHT	PERPETUALLY	AMENDED	IMPENETRABLE
EYRIE	MARAUDING	DELL	LURE	HOARD
MUSTERING	RUNES	FREE SPACE	EXPEDITION	PLUNDER
TUNIC	EDDYING	ANTIQUITY	PRECISE	UNCANNY
LARDERS	QUAY	IMPLORE	DROUGHT	SEIZED

The Hobbit Vocabulary

ABOMINABLE	PERILOUS	ENMITY	REQUISITE	CONSPIRATOR
INEVITABLE	INFURIATE	REMUNERATION	ABSURD	REPOSE
BUSTLE	KIN	FREE SPACE	SUSPICION	DEPREDATIONS
PERISH	VAIN	GUARDIAN	WROUGHT	LOATHSOME
UNIMPEACHABLE	AUDACIOUS	MEMOIRS	QUEST	PINNACLE

The Hobbit Vocabulary

ANTIQUITY	HOARD	ENMITY	RANSOM	QUEST
WANING	VAIN	AMENDED	AUDACIOUS	LARDERS
MEMOIRS	GUARDIAN	FREE SPACE	DROUGHT	PINNACLE
UNIMPEACHABLE	BUSTLE	KIN	EXPEDITION	HART
EYRIE	WROUGHT	MUSTERING	ABOMINABLE	EDDYING

The Hobbit Vocabulary

INEVITABLE	REMUNERATION	HINDER	MARAUDING	SORCEROUS
DEPREDATIONS	LURE	REPOSE	RUNES	ABSURD
PREFER	CONSPIRATOR	FREE SPACE	DUBIOUS	WILY
PERISH	DELL	SEIZED	PERPETUALLY	IMPENETRABLE
TUNIC	PURSUING	PERILOUS	PLIGHT	SUSPICION

The Hobbit Vocabulary

IMPLORE	ABOMINABLE	SEIZED	ABSURD	PLUNDER
ASTONISHED	GUARDIAN	MEMOIRS	HART	CONSPIRATOR
EDDYING	DELL	FREE SPACE	KIN	ENMITY
MARAUDING	REPOSE	REMUNERATION	REQUISITE	BUSTLE
LURE	HINDER	PLIGHT	DEPREDATIONS	VAIN

The Hobbit Vocabulary

UNCANNY	ANTIQUITY	INFURIATE	AMENDED	SUSPICION
DROUGHT	HOARD	LARDERS	RANSOM	QUAY
DUBIOUS	MUSTERING	FREE SPACE	EYRIE	PREFER
PURSUING	PERISH	WILY	WANING	INEVITABLE
UNIMPEACHABLE	LOATHSOME	AUDACIOUS	PERILOUS	IMPENETRABLE

The Hobbit Vocabulary

LARDERS	LURE	QUEST	ANTIQUITY	PERISH
AMENDED	ASTONISHED	IMPENETRABLE	ABSURD	INFURIATE
TUNIC	IMPLORE	FREE SPACE	DELL	PLIGHT
LOATHSOME	PINNACLE	BUSTLE	KIN	WILY
REQUISITE	ENMITY	MUSTERING	RUNES	DEPREDATIONS

The Hobbit Vocabulary

REPOSE	HART	MARAUDING	PERPETUALLY	EDDYING
AUDACIOUS	HOARD	DROUGHT	PLUNDER	RANSOM
UNCANNY	SORCEROUS	FREE SPACE	PERILOUS	PRECISE
SEIZED	GUARDIAN	VAIN	PREFER	EXPEDITION
HINDER	HOIST	INEVITABLE	QUAY	REMUNERATION

The Hobbit Vocabulary

PURSUING	AUDACIOUS	QUEST	DROUGHT	RANSOM
QUAY	LURE	PLUNDER	HART	DEPREDATIONS
PERPETUALLY	SEIZED	FREE SPACE	WROUGHT	INEVITABLE
IMPENETRABLE	ABOMINABLE	TUNIC	EXPEDITION	AMENDED
RUNES	ABSURD	CONSPIRATOR	MUSTERING	SUSPICION

The Hobbit Vocabulary

UNCANNY	PREFER	GUARDIAN	HOARD	ASTONISHED
PERISH	PLIGHT	UNIMPEACHABLE	LOATHSOME	PRECISE
HOIST	ANTIQUITY	FREE SPACE	DUBIOUS	REQUISITE
SORCEROUS	EYRIE	PERILOUS	KIN	EDDYING
HINDER	WANING	LARDERS	IMPLORE	ENMITY

The Hobbit Vocabulary

HOARD	PREFER	QUEST	PINNACLE	DELL
DROUGHT	ENMITY	ABOMINABLE	PLUNDER	GUARDIAN
PURSUING	HOIST	FREE SPACE	UNIMPEACHABLE	INEVITABLE
EXPEDITION	ANTIQUITY	SUSPICION	PERISH	LARDERS
IMPLORE	WILY	DUBIOUS	ASTONISHED	KIN

The Hobbit Vocabulary

TUNIC	VAIN	EYRIE	QUAY	LURE
PLIGHT	RUNES	SEIZED	DEPREDATIONS	INFURIATE
UNCANNY	EDDYING	FREE SPACE	PRECISE	REQUISITE
HART	SORCEROUS	MUSTERING	PERILOUS	RANSOM
CONSPIRATOR	WANING	LOATHSOME	AUDACIOUS	ABSURD

The Hobbit Vocabulary

HART	SORCEROUS	LURE	PURSUING	KIN
ASTONISHED	PREFER	LOATHSOME	PLIGHT	IMPENETRABLE
PRECISE	AUDACIOUS	FREE SPACE	QUAY	BUSTLE
DROUGHT	VAIN	PERISH	UNCANNY	MARAUDING
ABOMINABLE	REQUISITE	RUNES	HINDER	WROUGHT

The Hobbit Vocabulary

INFURIATE	HOIST	SEIZED	WILY	MUSTERING
TUNIC	EYRIE	RANSOM	DEPREDATIONS	SUSPICION
MEMOIRS	EXPEDITION	FREE SPACE	AMENDED	DUBIOUS
REPOSE	ENMITY	LARDERS	GUARDIAN	CONSPIRATOR
PERPETUALLY	QUEST	INEVITABLE	PERILOUS	UNIMPEACHABLE

The Hobbit Vocabulary

ABOMINABLE	PERPETUALLY	EYRIE	KIN	SORCEROUS
IMPLORE	AUDACIOUS	UNIMPEACHABLE	UNCANNY	REMUNERATION
PLIGHT	WROUGHT	FREE SPACE	IMPENETRABLE	DEPREDATIONS
MARAUDING	HINDER	PURSUING	TUNIC	AMENDED
BUSTLE	WANING	DUBIOUS	GUARDIAN	MEMOIRS

The Hobbit Vocabulary

SEIZED	HOIST	EXPEDITION	SUSPICION	EDDYING
LOATHSOME	PINNACLE	CONSPIRATOR	REPOSE	WILY
DROUGHT	MUSTERING	FREE SPACE	INEVITABLE	QUAY
PERISH	LARDERS	PRECISE	VAIN	INFURIATE
ABSURD	HART	RANSOM	QUEST	PLUNDER

www.ingramcontent.com/pod-product-compliance
Lightning Source LLC
Chambersburg PA
CBHW081455070526
44586CB00019B/2362